THE COMPLETE

NINJA FOODI

COOKBOOK

FOR TWO

800 Quick and Easy Ninja Foodi Recipes for Busy People

By

Emily Cook

COPYRIGHT © 2022 BY Emily Cook

Without the prior written permission of the publisher, no part of this publication should be reproduced, distributed, or transmitted in any form or by any means, including photocopying, recording, or other electronic or mechanical methods. This publication is sold with the idea that the publisher is not required to render accounting, officially permitted, or otherwise, qualified services. Seek for the services

of a legal or professional, a practiced individual in the profession if advice is needed.

DISCLAIMER

The information contained in this book is geared for educational and entertainment purposes only. Strenuous efforts have been made towards providing accurate, up to date and reliable complete information. The information in this book is true and complete to the best of our knowledge. Neither the publisher nor the author takes

any responsibility for any possible consequences of reading or enjoying the recipes in

this book. The author and publisher disclaim any liability in connection with the use of information contained in this book. Under no circumstance will any legal responsibility or blame be apportioned against the author or publisher for any reparation, damages, or monetary loss due to the information herein, either directly or indirectly.

Table of Contents

Function Keys of Your Ninja Foodi:

Ninja Foodi comes with many buttons for optimum operation of the unit which includes steam, slow cook, pressure cook, sear/sauté button, air crisp, broil, bake /roast and keep warm, buttons respectively. It also has buttons for temperature and time controls, start/stop button. The buttons and their functions are shown below:

1. Pressure Cook:

This button helps you to cook your meal up to 4 hours using high or low pressure. As earlier said, it is possible to adjust the cooking time to 1-minute increment for 1 hour. When the time is up, you may increase the time to 5 minutes and begin to cook up to 4 hours. Hence you can make a whole lot of meals.

2. Air Crisp:

This function gives you an opportunity to adjust the temperature to either 300°F or 400°F and also adjust to increase the cooking time to 2 minutes for the highest cooking time of 1 hour. The air crisp button is used in cooking many dishes like chicken tenders, French fries etc. Pressure cooked food can be crisp using this button.

3. Bake/Roast:

This setting in the Ninja is good for making roasted meats and baked foods. For this function, the Ninja Foodi uses the air-frying lid. There is no problem if you set the cooking time to 1-minute increment for 1 hour. When the time is up, you may increase the time to 5 minutes and begin to cook up to 4 hours. After the hour mark, you can increase the time in five-minute increments and cook for up to four hours.

4. Steam:

It is possible to steam your veggies and other meals by putting the pressure lid on the Ninja Foodi with the sealing valve in the vent position.

5. Slow cook:

This button also makes use of the pressure lid with the sealing valve in the vent position. It is possible for you to slow cook low or slow cook high. The cooking time can also be adjusted to 15 minutes increment for up to 12 hours. It is advisable to use the slow cook mode when cooking meals like stews, soup or pot roasts.

6. Sear/Sauté:

This button on the Ninja Foodi does not make use of the lid. It only has a temperature setting of 5 different modes respectively. These includes: medium, medium-high, high, low or medium-low, setting. Foods can be browned after cooking or before cooking. The button can also be used to make different kinds of sauces, gravies. This button functions the same as you would sear or sauté using your stovetop.

Steps on How to Use Your Ninja Foodi:

This appliance is a very friendly and easy-to-use kitchen unit.

For Ninja Foodi pressure cooker:

1. Always put your foods in the inner pot of the Ninja Foodi or you put your food in the Air Fryer basket. This is basically good for meats.

2. Press the power on function.

3. Close lid in place. Do not put the one that is attached.

4. Set the top steam valve to seal position and press the pressure function.

5. Adjust the temperature to either high or low using the + or − buttons respectively.

6. Set the cooking time using the + or − buttons.

7. Press Start button.

8. The Ninja Foodi will take a little time to reach pressure and then will count the number of minutes until it reaches zero minute.

For Ninja Foodi Air Fryer:

1. Make use of the lid that is attached.

2. Place the Air Fryer cooking basket inside the Ninja Foodi inner pot.

3. Place your food inside the cooking basket.

4. Lock the attached lid and switch on the Ninja Foodi by pressing the button at the bottom.

5. Push the air crisp button.

6. Select the temperature you want to use by pressing the + and − buttons.

7. Set the cooking time by pressing the + and − buttons.

8. Select start button.

Useful Tips & Tricks for Using Your Ninja Foodi

It is pertinent to inquire to know how to properly use a new appliance you bought. Ninja Foodi come with 2 distinct lids. One is for the electric pressure cooker while the other one is for the Air Fryer lid. It is possible to use both lids in on food. Immediately the pressure cooker is done, remove the pressure cooker lid and put the Air Fryer lid. This helps to crisp your food. Every new kitchen appliance you get comes with an operational manual to guide you on the proper usage of the unit. Below are some few tips for the proper usage of your Ninja Foodi:

1. Whenever you want to spray cooking spray on the inner pot of your Ninja Foodi, do not use aerosol cooking spray.

2. Try to use the recommended amount of water or broth if you are using the pressure-cooking button. Wrong usage of water may not give you the desired result.

3. When you are not using your Ninja Foodi, unplug from any power source so as to avoid the appliance switch on by itself even when you did not press the power on button.

4. It is not advisable to use your Ninja Foodi on your stove top. This can easily damage the unit.

Ninja Foodi Troubleshooting Tips

Every electronic appliance sometimes has trouble shooting or shows a faulty message on the display. Below are some of the major trouble shooting or problems you could find on your Ninja Foodi.

1. My appliance is taking a long time to come to pressure. Why?

It is important to know how long it takes your Ninja Foodi to come to pressure. Base on a particular temperature you choose, cooking time may vary. Temperature of the cooking pot at the moment of cooking including the amount of ingredients also makes cooking time to vary. If the cooking time is taking a longer time than necessary, make sure your silicone ring is fully seated and flush against the lid, make sure the pressure lid is fully closed and set the pressure release valve to seal position.

2. Why is the cooking time counting slowly?

You have to make sure you set the time correctly. Check if you did not use hours instead of minutes. Note that the HH stands for hours while the MM stands for minutes on the display window respectively. You can increase or decrease the cooking time.

3. How do I know when the appliance is pressurizing?

When the appliance is building pressure, the rotating lights will display on the display window. When you are using steam or pressure mode, light will rotate on the display screen. It means the appliance is preheating. Immediately the preheating process finishes, the normal cooking time starts counting.

4. When I'm using the steam mode, my unit is bringing out a lot of steam.

During cooking, steam releasing on the pressure release valve is normal. It is advisable to allow the pressure release valve in the vent position for Steam, Slow Cook, and Sear or Sauté mode.

5. Why can't I take off the pressure lid?

The Ninja Foodi has to be depressurized before the pressure lid can be opened. This is one of the safety measures put by the manufacturer. In order to do a quick pressure release, set the pressure release valve to the vent position. Immediately the pressure is released completely, the lid will be ready to open.

6. Do I need to lose the pressure release valve?

The answer is yes. You have to loosen the pressure release valve. It helps to circulate pressure through some release of small amount of steam while cooking is done for the result to be excellent.

Ninja Foodi Frequently Asked Questions and Answers:

Question 1: Can I deep fry chicken with this appliance?

Answer: Yes, it is possible. You can cook a chicken in your Ninja Foodi. This is a new modern way of cooking that can tender your food and progress to crisping the food using hot air and give you a crispy result.

Question 2: Can I Take My Ninja Pot from the Refrigerator and Put directly in the appliance?

Answer: Yes, you can do it if your pot was in the refrigerator.

Question 3: Can the Pot enter under the Broiler or the Oven?

Answer: Yes. It is possible but you have to be extra careful while putting or taking the pot out from the Ninja Foodi. It is only the lid that you do not need to put under the oven or the broiler.

Question 4: Can the Baking or cooking pan enter under the oven?

Answer: Yes. It is very possible and good to put the cooking pan under the oven. You just need to be careful while inserting the pan.

Question 5: Can I use the buffet settings to cook?

Answer: NO. It is not advisable to do that because the buffet function is just to keep temperature that is above 140°F when the food has been cooked to 165°F.

Question 6: What is the meaning of One-pot Meal Cooking?

Answer: These are important family meal that could be ready within 30 minutes time. The one pot helps in a quick clean up.

Question 7: What differentiate model op301 from model op305?

Answer: Model OP305 has the Dehydrate button while model OP301 has no dehydrate button. That's the major difference.

Question 8: Can you can food with Ninja Foodi?

Answer: No, you will not be able to can food with this appliance. You can only do it if you have a pressure canner can.

Question 9: Why is the time beeper not beeping?

Answer: You can check the volume level.

Question 10: Can I put frozen pork loin in my Ninja Foodi?

Answer: Yes. It is possible to do that. Frozen foods can be cooked with this appliance.

Question 11: If the Ninja foodi displays water, what is the meaning?

Answer: It means that you need to put more water into the Ninja Foodi. If at a point of putting more water and the error still show up, contact the customer care on 877581-7375.

Question 12: Can meat and cheese vegetables be cooked with this appliance?

Answer: No. Ninja Foodi was not meant for canning of foods. So, it will not work for you.

Ninja Foodi Pressure Releasing Methods:

This process is ideal for stopping all cooking process in order to avoid the food getting burnt. Foods like corn or broccoli etc. are ideal for this pressure releasing. There are two types of pressure release namely: Quick and natural pressure release.

1. **How to do a Ninja Foodi Quick Release**

Immediately the cooking time is up, keep the venting knob on Venting Position to enable Ninja Foodi quickly release the pressure inside the pressure cooker. To release all the pressure, it normally takes some few minutes. Before you open the lid, wait until the valve drops.

2. **How to do a Ninja Foodi Natural Release**

Immediately the cooking time is up, you have to wait until the valve drops and the lid is opened. In order to make sure all the pressure is released before opening the lid, keep the venting knob on Venting Position. This particular pressure release technique normally takes about 10 – 25 minutes but it depends on the amount of food in your cooker. To do the 10 – 15 minutes pressure release, when the cooking time is up, wait 10 – 15 minutes before moving the Venting Knob from Sealing Position to Venting Position so as to enable the remaining pressure to be released. Do not fail to wait for the floating valve to drop before you open the lid.

BREAKFAST RECIPES

Pumpkin Steel Cut Oatmeal

Preparation time: 10 minutes

Cooking time: 15 minutes

Overall time: 25 minutes

Serves: 2 to 4 people

Recipe Ingredients:

- ½ cup of pumpkin seeds, toasted
- 1 cup of pumpkin puree
- 2 cups steel cut oats
- 3 cups water
- 1 tbsp of butter
- 3 tablespoons of maple syrup
- ¼ teaspoon of cinnamon
- ½ teaspoon of salt

Cooking Instructions:

1. Melt the butter on Sear/Sauté mode, in cinnamon, oats, salt, pumpkin puree and water.

2. Seal the pressure lid, choose Pressure, set to High, and set the timer to 10 minutes and press the start button.

3. When cooking cycle is complete, do a quick pressure release. Open the lid and stir in maple syrup and top with toasted pumpkin seeds to serve.

Bacon and Sausage Cheesecake

Preparation time: 10 minutes

Cooking time: 15 minutes

Overall time: 25 minutes

Serves: 2 to 4 people

Recipe Ingredients:

- 8 eggs, cracked into a bowl
- 8 ounces of breakfast sausage; chopped /240g
- 4 slices of bread, cut into ½ -inch cubes
- 1 large green bell pepper; chopped
- 1 large red bell pepper; chopped
- 1 cup of chopped green onion /130g
- ½ cup of milk /125ml
- 2 cups of water /500ml
- 1 cup of grated Cheddar cheese /130g
- 3 bacon slices; chopped
- 1 teaspoon of red chili flakes /5g
- Salt and black pepper to taste

Cooking Instructions:

1. Add the eggs, sausage chorizo, bacon slices, green and red bell peppers, green onion, chili flakes, cheddar cheese, salt, pepper, and milk to a bowl.

2. Use a whisk to beat them together. Grease a Bundt pan with cooking spray and pour the egg mixture into it.

3. Drop the bread slices in the egg mixture all around while using a spoon to push them into the mixture.

4. Open the Ninja Foodi, pour in water, and fit the rack at the center of the pot. Place Bundt pan on the rack and seal the pressure lid.

5. Select Pressure mode on High pressure for about 6 minutes, and press Start/Stop. Once the timer is off, press the Start/Stop button and do a quick pressure release.

6. Run a knife around the egg in the Bundt pan, close the crisping lid and cook for another 4 minutes on Bake/Roast function at 380°F

7. When ready, place a serving plate on the Bundt pan, and then, turn the egg Bundt over. Use a knife to cut the egg into slices. Serve with a sauce of your choice.

Cheesy Bacon Grits

Preparation time: 10 minutes

Cooking time: 10 minutes

Overall time: 20 minutes

Serves: 2 to 4 people

Recipe Ingredients:

- 3 slices of smoked bacon; diced
- 1 cup of ground Grits /130g
- 1 ½ cups of grated Cheddar cheese /195g
- ½ cup of water /125ml
- ½ cup of milk /125ml
- 2 teaspoons of butter /30g
- Salt and black pepper

Cooking Instructions:

1. To preheat the Ninja Foodi, select Sear/Sauté function and set to HIGH pressure. Cook bacon until crispy, for about 5 minutes and set aside.

2. Add the grits, butter, milk, water, salt, and pepper to the pot and stir using a spoon. Close the pressure lid and secure the pressure valve.

3. Choose the Pressure mode and cook for about 3 minutes on High mode and press the Start/Stop button.

4. Once the timer has ended, turn the vent handle and do a quick pressure release. Add in cheddar cheese and give the pudding a good stir with the same spoon.

5. Close crisping lid, press the Bake/Roast button and cook for about 8 minutes on 370°F.

6. When ready, dish the cheesy grits into serving bowls and spoon over the crisped bacon. Serve right away with toasted bread.

French Dip Sandwiches

Preparation 30 minutes

Cooking time: 1 hour 5 minutes

Overall time: 1 hour 35 minutes

Serves: 2 to 4 people

Recipe Ingredients:

- 2 ½ lb. of beef roast /1125g
- 2 tablespoons of olive oil /30ml
- 1 onion; chopped
- 4 garlic cloves; sliced
- ½ cup of dry red wine /125ml
- 2 cups of beef broth stock /500ml
- 1 teaspoon of dried oregano /5g
- 16 slices of Fontina cheese
- 8 split hoagie rolls

Cooking Instructions:

1. Generously apply pepper and salt to the beef for seasoning. Warm oil on Sear/Sauté and brown the beef for about 2 to 3 minutes per side. Set aside on a plate.

2. Add onions and cook for about 3 minutes, until translucent. Mix in garlic and cook for one a minute until soft. To the Foodi, add red wine to deglaze.

3. Scrape the cooking surface to remove any browned sections of the food using a wooden spoon's flat edge.

4. Mix in beef broth and take back the juices and beef to your pressure cooker. Over the meat, scatter some oregano.

5. Seal the pressure lid, choose Pressure, set to High, and set the timer to 50 minutes; press Start. Release pressure naturally for about 10 minutes. Transfer the beef to a cutting board and slice. Roll the sliced beef and add a topping of onions.

6. Each sandwich should be topped with 2 slices fontina cheese. Place the sandwiches in the pot, close the crisping lid and select Air Crisp.

7. Adjust the temperature to 360°F and the time to 3 minutes. Press the Start button. When cooking is complete, the cheese should be cheese melt.

Paprika Shirred Eggs

Preparation time: 10 minutes

Cooking time: 10 minutes

Overall time: 20 minutes

Serves: 1 to 3 people

Recipe Ingredients:

- 4 eggs; divided
- 4 slices of ham
- 2 tablespoons of heavy cream /30ml
- 3 tablespoons of Parmesan cheese /45g
- ¼ teaspoon of pepper /1.25g
- 2 teaspoons of butter; for greasing /10g
- 2 teaspoons of chopped chives /10g
- ¼ teaspoon of paprika /1.25g

Cooking Instructions:

1. Grease a pie pan with the butter. Arrange the ham slices on the bottom of the pan to cover it completely. Use more slices if needed.

2. Whisk one egg along with the heavy cream, salt, and pepper, in a small bowl. Pour the mixture over the ham slices.

3. Crack the other eggs over the ham. Scatter Parmesan cheese over, close the crisping lid and cook for about 14 minutes on Air Crisp mode at 320°F

4. Sprinkle with paprika and garnish with chives.

Maple Giant Pancake

Preparation time: 10 minutes

Cooking time: 20 minutes

Overall time: 30 minutes

Serves: 2 to 4 people

Recipe Ingredients:

- 3 cups of flour /390g
- ⅓ cup of olive oil /84ml
- ⅓ cup of sparkling water /84ml
- ¾ cup of sugar /98g
- 5 eggs
- 2 tablespoons of maple syrup /30ml
- ⅓ teaspoon of salt /1.67g
- 1 ½ teaspoon of baking soda /7.5g
- A dollop of whipped cream to serve

Cooking Instructions:

1. Start by pouring the flour, sugar, eggs, olive oil, sparkling water, salt, and baking soda into a food processor and blend until smooth.

2. Pour the batter into the Ninja Foodi and let it sit in there for about 15 minutes. Close the lid and secure the pressure valve.

3. Select the Pressure mode on Low pressure for about 10 minutes. Press the Start/Stop button.

4. Once the timer goes off, press the Start/Stop button, quick-release the pressure valve to let out any steam and open the lid.

5. Gently run a spatula around the pancake to let lose any sticking. Once ready, slide the pancake onto a serving plate and drizzle with maple syrup.

6. Top with the whipped cream to serve

Deviled Eggs

Preparation 10 minutes

Cooking time: 10 minutes

Overall time: 20 minutes

Serves: 2 to 4 people

Recipe Ingredients:

- 10 large eggs
- ¼ cup of cream cheese /32.5ml
- ¼ cup of mayonnaise /62.5ml
- 1 cup of water /250ml
- ¼ tsp of chili powder /1.25g
- Salt and ground black pepper to taste

Cooking Instructions:

1. Add water to the Foodi's pot, insert the eggs into the steamer basket; place into the pot.

2. Seal the pressure lid, choose Pressure, set to High, and set the timer to 5 minutes. Press the Start button. When it is ready, release the pressure quickly.

3. Drop eggs into an ice bath to cool for about 5 minutes. Press Start. Peel eggs and halve them.

4. Transfer yolks to a bowl and use a fork to mash; stir in cream cheese, and mayonnaise.

5. Add pepper and salt for seasoning. Ladle yolk mixture into egg white halves.

Sweet Bread Pudding

Preparation 15 minutes

Cooking time: 30 minutes

Overall time: 45 minutes

Serves: 1 to 3 people

Recipe Ingredients:

- 8 slices of bread
- 2 eggs
- ¼ cup of sugar /32.5g
- ¼ cup of honey /62.5ml
- 1 cup of milk /250ml
- ½ cup of buttermilk /125ml
- 4 tablespoons of raisins /60g
- 2 tablespoons chopped hazelnuts /30g
- 2 tablespoons of butter, softened /30g
- ½ teaspoon of vanilla extract /2.5ml
- Cinnamon for garnish

Cooking Instructions:

1. Beat the eggs along with the buttermilk, honey, milk, vanilla, sugar, and butter.

2. Stir in raisins and hazelnuts. Cut the bread into cubes and place it in a bowl. Pour the milk mixture over the bread.

3. Let it soak for about 10 minutes. Close the crisping lid and cook the bread pudding for about 25 minutes on Roast mode.

4. Leave the dessert to cool for about 5 minutes, then invert onto a plate and sprinkle with cinnamon to serve.

Prosciutto Egg Bake

Preparation time: 15 minutes

Cooking time: 30 minutes

Overall time: 45 minutes

Serves: 2 to 4 people

Recipe Ingredients:

- 8 oz. of prosciutto; chopped
- 1 cup of shredded Monterey Jack cheese
- 1 cup of water
- 1 cup of whole milk
- 1 orange bell pepper, seeded and chopped
- 4 eggs
- 1 teaspoon of salt
- 1 teaspoon of freshly ground black pepper

Cooking Instructions:

1. Break the eggs into a bowl, pour in the milk, salt, and black pepper and whisk until combined.

2. Stir in the Monterey Jack Cheese. Put the bell pepper and prosciutto in the cake pan.

3. Then, pour over the egg mixture, cover the pan with aluminum foil and put on the reversible rack.

4. Put the rack in the pot and pour in the water. Seal the pressure lid, choose pressure and set to High. Set the time to 20 minutes and press the Start/Stop button.

5. When done cooking, do a quick pressure release and carefully remove the lid that is after the pressure has completely escaped.

6. When baking is complete, take the pan out of the pot and set it on a heatproof surface, and cool for about 5 minutes.

Raspberry and Vanilla Pancake

Preparation time: 5 minutes

Cooking time: 10 minutes

Overall time: 15 minutes

Serves: 2 to 4 people

Recipe Ingredients:

- ½ cup of frozen raspberries, thawed
- 3 eggs, beaten
- 1 cup of brown sugar
- 2 cups of all-purpose flour
- 1 cup of milk
- 2 tablespoons of maple syrup
- 1 teaspoon of baking powder
- 1 ½ teaspoon vanilla extract
- Pinch of salt
- Cooking spray

Cooking Instructions:

1. In a bowl, mix the sifted flour, baking powder, salt, milk, eggs, vanilla extract, sugar, and maple syrup, until smooth.

2. Gently stir in the raspberries. Grease the basket of your Ninja Foodi with cooking spray.

3. Drop the batter into the basket. Close the crisping lid and cook for about 10 minutes on Air Crisp mode at 390°F

4. Serve the pancake right away.

Very Berry Puffs

Preparation time: 10 minutes

Cooking time: 10 minutes

Overall time: 20 minutes

Serves: 1 to 3 people

Recipe Ingredients:

- 3 pastry dough sheets
- 2 cups of cream cheese /260g 1 tbsp honey /15ml
- 2 tablespoons of mashed raspberries /30g
- 2 tablespoons of mashed strawberries /30g
- ¼ teaspoon of vanilla extract /1.25ml

Cooking Instructions:

1. Divide the cream cheese between the dough sheets and spread it evenly.

2. In a small bowl, combine the berries, honey, and vanilla. Divide the mixture between the pastry sheets. Pinch the ends of the sheets, to form puff.

3. You can seal them by brushing some water onto the edges, or even better, use egg wash.

4. Lay the puffs into a lined baking dish. Place the dish into the Ninja Foodi, close the crisping lid and cook for about 15 minutes on Air Crisp mode at 370 °F.

5. Once the timer beeps, check the puffs to ensure they're puffed and golden. Serve warm.

Toasted Bagel

Preparation time: 5 minutes

Cooking time: 5 minutes

Overall time: 10 minutes

Serves: 1 to 3 people

Recipe Ingredients:

- 1 bagel
- 2 tablespoons of butter, softened /30g
- 1 tablespoon of Parmesan cheese /15g
- 1 teaspoon of dried basil /5g
- 1 teaspoon of dried parsley /5g
- 1 teaspoon of garlic powder /5g
- Salt and pepper, to taste

Cooking Instructions:

1. Cut the bagel in half. Place in the Ninja Foodi, close the crisping lid and cook for about 3 minutes on Air Crisp mode at 370°F.

2. Combine the butter, Parmesan, garlic, basil, and parsley, in a small bowl. Season with salt and pepper, to taste. Spread the mixture onto the toasted bagel.

3. Return the bagel to the Ninja Foodi, and cook for an additional 3 minutes on Roast mode.

4. Serve with tangy tomato relish on the side.

Cheesy Ham Sandwich

Preparation time: 5 minutes

Cooking time: 5 minutes

Overall time: 10 minutes

Serves: 1 to 3 people

Recipe Ingredients:

- 2 slices of American cheese
- 2 slices of bread
- 1 slice of ham
- 2 teaspoons of butter

Cooking Instructions:

1. Spread 1 teaspoon of butter on the outside of each of the bread slices.

2. Place one cheese slice on the inside of one bread slice, top with ham slice and another cheese slice. Cover with the second bread slice to create the sandwich.

3. Place into the Ninja Foodi basket, close the crisping lid and cook for about 4 minutes on Air Crisp mode at 370°F

4. Flip the sandwich and cook for about 4 minutes. When the timer beeps, remove the sandwich, cut diagonally.

5. Serve immediately with ketchup or chutney.

Cranberry-Raspberry Chia Oatmeal

Preparation time: 10 minutes

Cooking time: 20 minutes

Overall time: 30 minutes

Serves: 2 to 4 people

Recipe Ingredients:

- 2 raspberries; sliced
- ½ cup of dried cranberries, plus more for garnish
- 2 cups of old-fashioned oatmeal
- 3¾ cups of water
- ¼ cup of plain vinegar
- 1 tablespoon of cinnamon powder
- ½ teaspooon of nutmeg powder
- ½ teaspoon of vanilla extract
- ⅛ teaspoon of salt
- Honey; for topping

Cooking Instructions:

1. Combine the oatmeal, water, vinegar, nutmeg, cinnamon, vanilla, cranberries, raspberries, and salt in the pot.

2. Seal the pressure lid, hit Pressure, set to High, and set the timer to 11 minutes. Press Start/Stop to start cooking the oats.

3. When the timer has ended, perform a natural pressure release for about 10 minutes, then a quick pressure release to let off any remaining pressure.

4. Carefully open the lid. Stir the oatmeal, drizzle with honey and more dried cranberries, and serve immediately.

Veggie Salmon Balls

Preparation time: 10 minutes

Cooking time: 30 minutes

Overall time: 40 min

Serves: 2 to 4 people

Recipe Ingredients:

- 2 (5 ounces) packs of steamed salmon flakes
- 3 large potatoes, cut into chips
- 1 Red onion; chopped
- 3 eggs, cracked into a bowl
- 1 cup of breadcrumbs
- ¼ cup of chopped parsley
- 4 tablespoons of butter; divided
- 4 tablespoons mayonnaise
- 2 tablespoons of olive oil
- 1 red bell pepper, seeded and chopped
- 1 teaspoon of garlic powder
- 2 teaspoons of Worcestershire sauce /10ml
- Salt and black pepper to taste

Cooking Instructions:

1. Turn on the Ninja Foodi and select Sear/Sauté mode on High pressure. Heat the oil and add half of the butter.

2. Once it has melted, add the onions and the chopped red bell peppers. Cook for about 6 minutes while stirring occasionally and press the Start/Stop button.

3. In a mixing bowl, add salmon flakes, sautéed red bell pepper and onion, breadcrumbs, eggs, mayonnaise, Worcestershire sauce, garlic powder, salt, pepper, and parsley.

4. Use a spoon to mix well while breaking the salmon into the tiny pieces. Use your hands to mold 4 patties out of the mixture.

5. Add the remaining butter to melt, and when melted, add the patties. Fry for about 4 minutes, flipping once.

6. Then, close the crisping lid, select Bake/Roast mode and bake for 4 minutes on 320°F.

7. Remove them onto a wire rack to rest. Serve the cakes with a side of lettuce and potato salad with a mild drizzle of herb vinaigrette.

LUNCH RECIPES

Chicken Noodle Soup

Preparation time: 10 minutes

Cooking time: 30 minutes

Overall time: 40 minutes

Serves: 2 to 4 people

Recipe Ingredients:

- 1 lb. of chicken breasts, bone-in, skin-on
- 8 oz. of extra-wide dry egg noodles
- 1 onion, minced
- 1 turnip; chopped
- 1 bay leaf
- 3 cloves of garlic, minced
- 6 cups of chicken broth /1500ml
- 1 cup of celery rib; chopped /130g
- 1 tablespoon of olive oil /15ml
- 1 tablespoon of dry basil /15g
- Salt and ground black pepper to taste

Cooking Instructions:

1. Set your Foodi to the Sear/Sauté function, set to Medium High, and choose Start/Stop to preheat the pot.

2. Warm olive oil; stir in garlic and onion and cook for about 3 minutes until soft. Mix in celery, bay leaf, basil, and turnip.

3. Add 3 cups of chicken broth to the pot and deglaze. Scrape any brown bits from the pan's bottom and add chicken.

4. Seal the pressure lid, choose Pressure, set to High, and set the timer to 10 minutes; press the Start button.

5. When ready, naturally release the pressure for about 7 minutes. Transfer chicken breasts to another bowl.

6. Do away with the skin and bones. Using two forks, shred the meat. Set the cooker to the Sear/Sauté function.

7. Transfer the chicken back to the pot; add the noodles and the remaining chicken stock.

8. Simmer the stock and cook for about 10 minutes until noodles are done. Add pepper and salt for seasoning.

Minestrone Soup

Preparation time: 10 minutes

Cooking time: 15 minutes

Overall time: 25 minutes

Serves: 2 to 4 people

Recipe Ingredients:

- 1 yellow onion; diced
- 1 (14 oz.) can of Navy beans, rinsed and drained
- 1 (28 oz.) can of diced tomatoes
- 1 (6 oz.) can of tomato paste
- 2 cloves of garlic, minced
- 1 carrot, peeled and diced
- 2 bay leaves
- 1 green bell pepper; chopped
- 3 cups of chicken broth
- 1 cup of celery; chopped
- 2 cups of kale
- ½ cup of white rice
- ¼ cup of Parmesan cheese
- 2 tablespoon of olive oil
- ½ teaspoon of dried oregano
- ½ teaspoon of dried parsley
- ½ teaspoon of dried thyme
- ½ teaspoon of salt
- ¼ teaspoon of ground black pepper

Cooking Instructions:

1. Warm olive oil on the Sear/Sauté function and stir in carrot, celery and onion.

2. Cook for about 5 to 6 minutes until soft. Add garlic and bell pepper and cook for about 2 minutes as you stir until aromatic.

3. Stir in pepper, thyme, stock, salt, parsley, oregano, tomatoes, bay leaves, and tomato paste to dissolve; mix in rice.

4. Seal the pressure lid, choose Pressure, set to High, and set the timer to 15 minutes; press the Start button.

5. Once ready, do a quick pressure release. Add kale to the liquid and stir. Use residual heat in slightly wilting the greens.

6. Get rid of bay leaves. Stir in navy beans. Serve topped with parmesan cheese.

Acorn Squash Soup

Preparation time: 10 minutes

Cooking time: 15 minutes

Overall time: 25 minutes

Serves: 2 to 4 people

Recipe Ingredients:

- 1 (2 lb.) acorn squash, peeled, seeded; chopped /60
- 2 carrots, peeled and diced
- 1 onion; diced
- 4 cups of vegetable broth /1000ml
- 1/3 cup of sour cream /84ml
- ½ cup of coconut milk /125ml
- 2 tablespoons of butter /30g
- ½ teaspoon of ground cinnamon /2.5g
- ¼ teaspoon of chili pepper /1.25g
- A pinch of salt

Cooking Instructions:

1. Set Foodi to the Sear/Sauté function, set to Medium High, and choose Start/Stop to preheat. Melt butter; add onion and cook for about 3 minutes until soft.

2. Add in carrots, cinnamon, squash, salt, and chili pepper and stir-fry for about 2 minutes until fragrant.

3. Add the stock to the vegetable mixture. Seal the pressure lid, choose Pressure, set to High, and set the timer to 12 minutes; press Start.

4. Quick-release the pressure. Add soup to a food processor and puree to obtain a smooth consistency.

5. Take the soup back To the Foodi, stir in coconut milk until you get a consistent color. Divide into serving bowls.

6. Serve hot with a dollop of sour cream.

Hearty Vegetable Soup

Preparation time: 10 minutes

Cooking time: 20 minutes

Overall time: 30 minutes

Serves: 2 to 4 people

Recipe Ingredients:

- 28 oz. of canned tomatoes /840g
- 15 oz. of canned garbanzo beans, rinsed and drained 450g
- 1 cup of frozen green peas /130g
- 5 cups of chicken broth /1250ml
- 1 cup of celery; chopped /130g
- ¼ cup of parmesan cheese, grated /32.5g
- 1 onion; chopped
- 2 carrots, peeled and chopped
- 2 bay leaves
- 2 cloves of garlic, minced
- 2 turnips, peeled and chopped
- 1 sprig of fresh sage
- 2 tablespoons of olive oil /30ml
- Salt and ground black pepper to taste

Cooking Instructions:

1. Set your Foodi to the Sear/Sauté function, set to Medium High, and choose the Start/Stop button to preheat the pot.

2. Warm oil; stir in celery, carrots, and onion and cook for about 4 minutes until soft. Add in garlic and cook for about 30 seconds until crispy.

3. Into the Foodi, add vegetable broth, parsnip, garbanzo beans, bay leaves, tomatoes, pepper, salt, peas, and sage.

4. Seal the pressure lid, press Pressure, set to High, and set the timer to 12 minutes; press the Start button.

5. Once done, release remaining pressure quickly. Serve topped with parmesan cheese.

Hawaiian Pizza

Preparation time: 5 minutes

Cooking time: 10 minutes

Overall time: 15 minutes

Serves: 1 to 3 people

Recipe Ingredients:

- 2 tortillas
- 8 thin pineapple slices
- 8 ham slices
- 8 mozzarella slices
- 2 tablespoons of tomato sauce /30ml
- Fresh basil leaves; chopped

Cooking Instructions:

1. Spread each tortilla with tomato sauce. Scatter over the ham, pineapple, and mozzarella.

2. Place the pizza into your Ninja Foodi basket, close the crisping lid and cook for about 10 minutes on Air Crisp mode.

3. When the timer beeps, remove and allow to sit for about 2 minutes before slicing. Sprinkle the basil over and serve with napkins.

Cheesy Ham Eggplant Boats

Preparation time: 7 minutes

Cooking time: 10 minutes

Overall time: 17 minutes

Serves: 1 to 3 people

Recipe Ingredients:

- 6 ham slices; chopped
- 1 cup of mozzarella cheese, shredded
- 2 eggplants
- 1 tsp. of dried parsley
- Cooking spray
- Salt and pepper, to taste

Cooking Instructions:

1. Grease the Ninja Foodi basket with cooking spray and set it aside.

2. Cut the eggplants lengthwise in half and scoop some of the flesh out, leaving the skin intact.

3. Season with salt and pepper, chop the scooped flesh and mix with mozzarella cheese, salt, and pepper.

4. Divide the cheese mixture between the eggplant halves. Cover with ham slices, and sprinkle with parsley.

5. Put the eggplant in the greased basket, close the crisping lid and cook for about 12 minutes on Air Crisp mode at 350°F.

6. Serve with a fresh salad.

Pumpkin Chipotle Soup

Preparation time: 5 minutes

Cooking time: 20 minutes

Overall time: 25 minutes

Serves: 2 to 4 people

Recipe Ingredients:

- 1 large butternut pumpkin, cut into small pieces
- 1 onion; chopped
- 2 chipotle peppers, seeded and finely minced
- 1 pinch of ground cinnamon
- 1 cup of half-and-half
- 4 cups of vegetable broth
- 1 tablespoon of olive oil
- ¼ teaspoon of grated nutmeg
- ¼ teaspoon of ground cloves
- 1 teaspoon of ground black pepper
- 1 teaspoon of salt

Cooking Instructions:

1. Warm oil on the Sear/Sauté function and sauté nutmeg, pepper, clove, cinnamon, and onion for about 3 to 5 minutes until translucent.

2. Add pumpkin and cook for about 5 minutes as you stir infrequently. Pour in the broth and add chipotle peppers and any remaining pumpkin.

3. Seal the pressure lid, choose Pressure, set to High, and set the timer to 10 minutes; press the Start button.

4. When ready, release pressure quickly. Stir in half-and-half and transfer to a blender to purée until you obtain a smooth consistency.

Creamy Mushroom and Quinoa Pilaf

Preparation time: 5 minutes

Cooking time: 15 minutes

Overall time: 20 minutes

Serves: 2 to 4 people

Recipe Ingredients:

- 1 onion; chopped
- 2 garlic cloves, smashed
- 1 carrot, peeled and chopped
- 1 stalk celery; diced
- ½ cup of heavy cream
- 1 cup of mushrooms; sliced
- 4 cups of vegetable broth
- 2 cups of quinoa, rinsed
- 3 tablespoons of butter
- 1 teaspoon of salt
- ½ teaspoon of dried thyme

Cooking Instructions:

1. Melt the butter on the Sear/Sauté function. Add onion, garlic, celery, and carrot, and cook for about 8 minutes until tender.

2. Mix in broth, thyme, quinoa, mushrooms, and salt. Seal the pressure lid, choose Pressure, set to High, and set the timer to 10 minutes; press Start.

3. When ready, release pressure quickly. Carefully open the lid and stir in heavy cream.

4. Cook for about 2 minutes to obtain a creamy consistency. Serve warm.

Leek and Potato Soup

Preparation time: 10 minutes

Cooking time: 20minutes

Overall time: 30 minutes

Serves: 2 to 4 people

Recipe Ingredients:

- 3 potatoes, peeled and cubed
- 3 leeks, white part only, thinly sliced
- 2 bay leaves
- 2 cloves of garlic, minced
- ½ cup of sour cream
- 4 cups of vegetable broth
- 2 tablespoons of butter
- 2 tablespoons of rosemary
- 2 tablespoons of fresh chives, to garnish
- Salt and ground black pepper to taste

Cooking Instructions:

1. Melt the butter on the Sear/Sauté function.

2. Stir in garlic and leeks and cook for about 3 to 4 minutes until soft. Stir in bay leaves, potatoes, and broth.

3. Seal the pressure lid, press Pressure, set to High, and set the timer to 15 minutes; press the Start button. When ready, release pressure quickly.

4. Remove the bay leaves and cobs and discard. Transfer soup to immersion blender and puree soup to obtain a smooth consistency.

5. Add pepper and salt for seasoning. Apply a topping of and freshly diced chives. Serve with sour cream.

Beef Broth

Preparation time: 10 minutes

Cooking time: 1 hour

Overall time: 1 hour 10 minutes

Serves: 2 to 4 people

Recipe Ingredients:

- 2 lb. of beef stew meat
- 2 red chilies, deseeded and chopped
- 2 carrots; chopped
- 4 garlic cloves
- 2 leeks; chopped
- 1 onion; chopped
- 2 cups of celery; chopped
- 8 cups of water
- 1 teaspoon of cider vinegar
- 1 teaspoon of fresh ginger, grated
- Salt to taste

Cooking Instructions:

1. In the Foodi, mix meat, celery, garlic carrots, leeks, onion, red chilies, and ginger.

2. Top with vinegar and water. Seal the pressure lid, choose Pressure, set to High, and set the timer to 45 minutes.

3. Press the Start button and release pressure naturally for about 10 minutes, then release the remaining pressure quickly.

4. Use a fine-mesh strainer to strain the broth into a bowl; add salt for seasoning. Serve or refrigerate using sealable containers.

Spicy Soup with Collard Greens

Preparation time: 5 minutes

Cooking time: 15 minutes

Overall time: 20 minutes

Serves: 2 to 4 people

Recipe Ingredients:

- 1 (1 lb.) package fresh collard greens, trimmed
- 1 red chilli; sliced to serve
- 10 oz. of ramen noodles
- 6 cups of chicken broth stock
- 1 cup of mushrooms; sliced
- A bunch of fresh cilantro; chopped to serve
- 2 tablespoons of soy sauce
- 1 tablespoon of olive oil
- 2 tablespoons garlic, minced
- 1 tablespoon of chili powder
- ½ teaspoon of ground ginger

Cooking Instructions:

1. Set your Foodi to the Sear/Sauté function and set to Medium High, and choose Start/Stop to preheat the pot.

2. Warm oil; stir in garlic and ginger and cook for about 2 minutes until soft. Add vegetable stock to the pot.

3. Mix in chili powder, ramen noodles and soy sauce. Seal the pressure lid, press Pressure, set to High, and set the timer to 10 minutes.

4. Press the Start button, when ready, release pressure quickly. Stir in collard greens until wilted.

5. Ladle the soup into serving bowls and add red chili and cilantro to serve.

Chicken Farro Soup

Preparation time: 10 minutes

Cooking time: 50 minutes

Overall time: 1 hour

Serves: 2 to 4 people

Recipe Ingredients:

- 4 boneless, skinless chicken thighs
- 1 large onion; sliced
- 2 celery stalks, cut into squares
- 1 bay leaf
- 3 large carrots; sliced
- 6 cups of chicken broth
- ¼ cup of white wine
- 1 cup of farro
- 1 tablespoon of olive oil
- 1 teaspoon of garlic powder
- 1 teaspoon of ground cumin
- 2 teaspoons of fresh parsley leaves to garnish 10g

Cooking Instructions:

1. Warm oil on Sear/Sauté. Brown the chicken on all sides, for about 6 minutes.

2. Transfer the chicken to a bowl. Into the pot, add wine to deglaze, scraping any brown bits present at the bottom of the cooker.

3. Mix the wine with farro, cumin, stock, onion, carrots, celery, garlic powder, and bay leaf.

4. Close the lid and turn steam vent to sealing. Seal the pressure lid, choose Pressure, set to High, and set the timer to 20 minutes.

5. Press the start button, when cooking is done, naturally release the pressure for about 10 minutes.

6. Divide between serving bowls and add parsley for garnish.

Italian Style Sausage Patties

Preparation time: 5 minutes

Cooking time: 15 minutes

Overall time: 20 minutes

Serves: 2 to 4 people

Recipe Ingredients:

- 1 pound of ground Italian sausage
- 1 egg, beaten
- ¼ cup of breadcrumbs
- ¼ tsp of garlic powder
- 1 tsp of dried parsley
- 1 tsp of red pepper Flakes
- ½ tsp of salt
- ¼ tsp of black pepper

Cooking Instructions:

1. Line the basket with parchment paper; set aside.

2. Combine all Ingredients in a large bowl. Use your hands to combine the mixture thoroughly.

3. Make patties out of the sausage mixture and arrange them on the basket. Close the crisping lid and cook for about 14 minutes on Air Crisp function at 350°F.

4. After 7 minutes, flip each patty. Once ready, remove and serve with tzatziki sauce.

Applesauce with Cinnamon

Preparation time: 15 minutes

Cooking time: 30 minutes

Overall time: 45 minutes

Serves: 2 to 4 people

Recipe Ingredients:

- 4 apples, cored; sliced
- ½ cup of water
- 1 teaspoon of honey
- 1 teaspoon of ground cinnamon

Cooking Instructions:

1. Add apples, cinnamon, water, and honey to your Foodi.

2. Seal the pressure lid, choose Pressure, set to High, and set the timer to 4 minutes; press Start.

3. Once ready, release pressure naturally for about 10 minutes. If you desire a chunky blend, stir vigorously.

4. For smooth applesauce, puree the mixture in a blender. Allow cooling before transferring in containers for storage.

Cream of Spinach and Mushroom Soup

Preparation time: 5 minutes

Cooking time: 20 minutes

Overall time: 25 minutes

Serves: 2 to 4 people

Recipe Ingredients:

- 8 Button Mushrooms; sliced
- 2 sweet potatoes, peeled and chopped
- 1 red onion; chopped
- 1 cup of creme fraiche
- 4 cups of vegetable stock
- 1 cup of spinach; chopped
- 2 tablespoons of white wine
- 1 tablespoon of olive oil
- 1 tablespoon of dry Porcini mushrooms, soaked and drained
- ½ teaspoon of sea salt
- ½ teaspoon of black pepper

Cooking Instructions:

1. Set your Foodi to the Sear/Sauté function, set to Medium High, and press the Start/Stop button to preheat the pot.

2. Add in olive oil and sliced mushrooms and cook for about 3 to 5 minutes until browning on both sides; set aside.

3. Add onion and spinach, and cook for about 3 to 5 minutes until onion is translucent.

4. Stir in chopped mushrooms, and cook for a further 5 minutes as you stir occasionally until golden brown.

5. Pour in wine to deglaze the bottom of the pot, scrape the bottom to remove browned bits. Cook for about 5 minutes until all the wine evaporates.

6. Mix in the remaining chopped fresh mushrooms, potatoes, soaked mushrooms, wine, vegetable stock, and salt.

7. Seal the pressure lid, choose Pressure, set to High, and set the timer to 5 minutes and press the start button.

8. Once cooking is complete, do a quick release. Add in pepper and creme fraiche to mix. Using an immersion blender, whizz the mixture until smooth.

9. Stir in the sautéed mushrooms. Add reserved mushrooms for garnish before serving.

POULTRY RECIPES

Chicken with Cilantro Rice

Preparation time: 20 minutes

Cooking time: 50 minutes

Overall time: 70 minutes

Serves: 2 to 4 people

Recipe Ingredients:

- 1 lb. of bone-in, skin-on chicken thighs
- 1 cup of basmati rice
- ¾ cup of chicken broth
- ½ cup of tomato sauce
- 1 red onion; diced
- 1 yellow bell pepper; diced
- 2 tablespoons of ghee divided
- 1 tablespoon of cayenne powder
- 1 teaspoon of ground cumin
- 1 teaspoon of Italian herb mix
- ½ teaspoon salt
- Chopped fresh cilantro, for garnish
- Lime wedges; for serving

Cooking Instructions:

1. Select the Sear/Sauté function, on the pot and set to Medium High. Select the Start/Stop button to preheat the pot.

2. Melt half of the ghee in the pot, and cook the onion for about 3 minutes, stirring occasionally, until softened.

3. Include the yellow bell pepper, cayenne pepper, cumin, herb mix, and salt, and cook for about 2 minutes more with frequent stirring.

4. Pour the rice, broth, and tomato sauce into the pot. Place the reversible rack in the higher position of the pot, which is over the rice.

5. Put the chicken on the rack. Seal the pressure lid, choose pressure, set to High, and set the time to 30 minutes.

6. Select the Start/Stop button to begin cooking the rice. When the time is over, perform a quick pressure release and carefully open the lid.

7. Brush the chicken thighs with the remaining 1 tablespoon of ghee. Close the crisping lid.

8. Choose Broil and set the time to 5 minutes. Press the Start/Stop button, when ready, check for your desired crispiness and remove the rack from the pot.

9. Plate the chicken, garnish with cilantro, and serve with lime wedges.

Mexican Style Green Chili Chicken

Preparation time: 10 minutes

Cooking time: 30 minutes

Overall time: 40 minutes

Serves: 2 to 4 people

Recipe Ingredients:

- 1½ lb. of boneless skinless chicken breasts
- 12 oz. of baby plum tomatoes, halved
- 2 jalapeño peppers, seeded and chopped
- 2 large serrano pepper, seeded and cut into chunks
- 2 large garlic cloves; minced
- ½ lime, juiced
- Tortilla chips
- 1 small onion; sliced
- ¼ cup of minced fresh cilantro
- ¾ cup of chicken stock
- ½ cup of shredded Cheddar Cheese
- 1 tablespoon of olive oil
- ½ teaspoon of salt
- ½ teaspoon of ground cumin
- 1 teaspoon of Mexican seasoning mix
- Cooking spray

Cooking Instructions:

1. Select the Sear/Sauté function on your Foodi and adjust to High. Press Start to preheat the inner pot.

2. Heat the olive oil add the plum tomatoes; cook without turning, for about 4 minutes.

3. Add the chicken stock while scraping the bottom of the pot to dissolve any browned bits. Stir in the cumin, Mexican seasoning, and salt.

4. Add the chicken, jalapeños, serrano pepper, garlic, onion, and half the cilantro. Seal the pressure lid, choose pressure.

5. Adjust the pressure to High and the cook time to 10 minutes. Press Start. Meanwhile, grease the reversible rack with cooking spray.

6. Fix the rack in the upper position of the pot. Cut out a circle of aluminum foil to fit the rack and place on the rack.

7. Lay on a single layer of tortilla chips, sprinkle with half of the Cheddar cheese and repeat with another layer of chips and cheese, set it aside.

8. After cooking, perform a natural pressure release for about 5 minutes. Take out the chicken from the pot and set it aside.

9. Then, with an immersion blender, purée the vegetables into the sauce. Shred the chicken with two forks and return the pieces to the sauce.

10. Add the remaining cilantro and the lime juice. Taste and adjust the seasoning and carefully transfer the rack of chips to the pot.

11. Close the crisping lid and Choose Air Crisp; adjust the temperature to 375°F and the time to 5 minutes and press the start.

12. When done cooking, open the lid. Carefully take out the rack and pour the chips into a platter. Serve the chili in bowls with the chips on the side.

Chicken with Tomato Salsa

Preparation time: 10 minutes

Cooking time: 20 minutes

Overall time: 30 minutes

Serves: 2 to 4 people

Recipe Ingredients:

- 4 chicken thighs; skinless but with bone
- 1 large red bell pepper, seeded and diced
- 1 large green bell pepper, seeded and diced
- 1 Red onion; diced
- 1 bay leaf
- ½ cup of chicken broth
- 1 cup of crushed tomatoes
- 1 tablespoon of chopped basil
- 4 tablespoons of olive oil
- ½ teaspoon of dried oregano
- Salt and black pepper to taste

Cooking Instructions:

1. Place the chicken on a clean flat surface and season with salt and pepper.

2. Select the Sear/Sauté function on High mode and heat the oil. Once heated add the chicken to brown on both sides for about 6 minutes.

3. Add the onions and peppers. Cook for about 5 minutes until nice and soft. Add bay leaf, salt, broth, pepper, and oregano.

4. Stir using a spoon, close the pressure lid, secure the pressure valve, and select Pressure mode on High for about 15 minutes.

5. Press the Start/Stop button. Once the timer has ended, do a natural pressure release for about 5 minutes.

6. Discard the bay leaf. Stir in tomatoes, close the crisping lid, select Broil mode and cook for about 25 minutes.

7. Dish the chicken with the sauce into a serving bowl and garnish with the chopped basil. Serve over a bed of steamed squash spaghetti.

Chicken Thighs with Thyme Carrot Roast

Preparation time: 10 minutes

Cooking time: 40 minutes

Overall time: 50 minutes

Serves: 2 to 4 people

Recipe Ingredients:

- 4 bone-in, skin-on chicken thighs
- 1 ½ cups of chicken broth
- 1 cup of basmati rice
- 2 carrots; chopped
- 2 tablespoons of melted butter
- 2 teaspoons of chopped fresh thyme
- 2 teaspoons of chicken seasoning
- 1 teaspoon of salt; divided

Cooking Instructions:

1. Pour the chicken broth and rice in the pot, put the reversible rack in the pot.

2. Arrange the chicken thighs on the rack, skin side up, and arrange the carrots around the chicken.

3. Put the pressure lid together and lock in the Seal position. Choose Pressure, set to High, and the time to 2 minutes.

4. Press the Start/Stop button to begin cooking the chicken. When done cooking, perform a quick pressure release, and carefully open the lid.

5. Brush the carrots and chicken with the melted butter. Season the chicken with the chicken seasoning and half of the salt.

6. Season the carrots with the thyme and remaining salt. Close the crisping lid; choose Broil and set the time to 10 minutes.

7. Press the Start/Stop buttonto begin crisping. When done cooking, check for your desired crispiness, and the turn the Foodi off.

8. Spoon the rice into serving plates, and serve the chicken and carrots over the rice.

Sesame Chicken Wings

Preparation time: 15 minutes

Cooking time: 50 minutes

Overall time: 65 minutes

Serves: 2 to 4 people

Recipe Ingredients:

- 24 chicken wings
- 2 garlic cloves; minced
- 2 tablespoons of honey
- 1 tablespoon of toasted sesame seeds
- 2 tablespoons of sesame oil
- 2 tablespoons of hot garlic sauce

Cooking Instructions:

1. Pour 1 cup of water into the Foodi's inner pot and place the reversible rack in the lower position of the pot.

2. Place the chicken wings on the rack. Seal the pressure lid, choose Pressure; adjust the pressure to High and the cook time to 10 minutes.

3. Press the Start button to begin cooking the chicken. While the wings cook, prepare the glaze.

4. In a large bowl, whisk the sesame oil, hot garlic sauce, honey, and garlic. After cooking, perform a quick pressure release, and carefully open the lid.

5. Remove the rack from the pot and empty the water in the pot. Return the pot to the base.

6. Close the crisping lid and Choose Air Crisp; adjust the temperature to 375°F and the time to 3 minutes to preheat the inner pot.

7. Press the Start button to begin, toss the wings in the sauce to properly coat. Put the wings in the Crisping Basket, leaving any excess sauce in the bowl.

8. Place the basket in the Foodi and close the crisping lid. Select the Air Crisp function and adjust the cook time to 15 minutes.

9. Press the Start button to commence crisping. After 8 minutes, open the lid and use tongs to turn the wings.

10. Close the lid to resume browning until the wings are crisp and the glaze set. Before serving, drizzle with any remaining sauce and sprinkle with the sesame seeds.

Lemon and Paprika Chicken Thighs

Preparation time: 6 minutes

Cooking time: 20 minutes

Overall time: 26 minutes

Serves: 2 to 4 people

Recipe Ingredients:

- 4 chicken thighs
- 1 lemon, zested and juiced
- 1 small onion; chopped
- 2 cloves of garlic; sliced
- ½ cup chicken broth
- 1 ½ tablespoons of heavy cream
- 1 ½ tablespoon of olive oil
- ½ teaspoon of garlic powder
- ½ teaspoon of red pepper flakes
- ½ teaspoon of smoked paprika
- 1 teaspoon of Italian Seasoning
- Salt and black pepper to taste
- Lemon slices to garnish
- Chopped parsley to garnish

Cooking Instructions:

1. Preheat the Foodi by selecting the Sear/Sauté function on Medium. Warm the olive oil and add the chicken thighs; cook to brown on each side for about 3 minutes.

2. Remove the browned chicken onto a plate. Melt the butter in the pot, then, add garlic, onions, and lemon juice.

3. Deglaze the bottom of the pot and cook for 1 minute. Add the Italian seasoning, chicken broth, lemon zest, and the chicken. Close the pressure lid, secure the pressure valve, select Pressure on High for about 10 minutes. Press the Start/Stop button.

4. When when the time is up, do a quick pressure release. Open the lid. Stir in the heavy cream. Close the crisping lid and select Broil mode.

5. Set the time to 5 minutes. Serve with the steamed kale and spinach mix. Garnish with the lemon's slices and parsley.

Herbed Chicken and Biscuit Chili.

Preparation time: 10 minutes

Cooking time: 80 minutes

Overall time: 90 minutes

Serves: 2 to 4 people

Recipe Ingredients:

- 1½ lb. of ground chicken /675g
- 1 package of refrigerated biscuits, at room temperature
- 1 onion; chopped
- 2 garlic cloves; minced
- 4 cups of chicken broth /1000ml
- 1 tablespoon of olive oil /15ml
- 1 tablespoon of ground cilantro /15g
- 1 tablespoon of dried oregano /15g
- ⅛ teaspoon of salt /0.625g
- ⅛ teaspoon of black pepper /0.625g

Cooking Instructions:

1. Select the Sear/Sauté function on the Foodi and set to Medium-High; press the Start/Stop button to preheat the pot.

2. Pour the oil, chicken, onion, and garlic into the inner pot and sauté until the onion is softened, for about 3 minutes.

3. Add the cilantro, oregano, broth, salt, and black pepper to the pot. Put the pressure lid together and lock in the Seal position.

4. Choose Pressure and set to High. Set the time to 10 minutes, then press the Start/Stop button to begin cooking.

5. When the time is over, perform a quick pressure release, and carefully open the lid. Spread the biscuits in a single layer over the chili.

6. Close the crisping lid. Choose Broil and set the time to 15 minutes. Press the Start/Stop button to commence browning.

7. When ready, remove the pot from the Foodi and place on a heat-resistant surface. Let the chili and biscuits rest for about 10 to 15 minutes before serving.

Turkey Enchilada Casserole

Preparation time: 10 minutes

Cooking time: 60 minutes

Overall time: 70 minutes

Serves: 2 to 4 people

Recipe Ingredients:

- 1 lb. of boneless; skinless turkey breasts
- 2 cups of shredded Monterey Jack cheese; divided
- 2 cups of enchilada sauce
- 1 yellow onion; diced
- 2 garlic cloves; minced
- 1 (15 oz.) can of pinto beans, drained and rinsed
- 1 (16 oz.) bag of frozen corn
- 8 tortillas, each cut into 8 pieces
- 1 tablespoon of butter
- ¼ teaspoon of salt
- ¼ teaspoon of freshly ground black pepper

Cooking Instructions:

1. Select the Sear/Sauté function on the pot and set to Medium High. Select the Start/Stop button to preheat the pot.

2. Melt the butter and cook the onion for about 3 minutes, stirring occasionally. Stir in the garlic and cook until fragrant, about 1 minute more.

3. Put the turkey and enchilada sauce in the pot, and season with salt and black pepper.

4. Stir to combine, seal the pressure lid, choose Pressure, set to High, and set the time to 15 minutes.

5. Press the Start/Stop button. When done cooking, perform a quick pressure release and carefully open the lid.

6. Shred the turkey with two long forks while being careful not to burn your hands. Mix in the pinto beans, tortilla pieces, corn, and half of the cheese to the pot.

7. Sprinkle the remaining cheese evenly on top of the casserole. Close the crisping lid. Choose Broil and set the time to 5 minutes.

8. Press the Start/Stop button to begin broiling. When ready, allow the casserole to
    sit for about 5 minutes before serving.

Chicken and Green Bean Coconut Curry

Preparation time: 12 minutes

Cooking time: 20 minutes

Overall time: 32 minutes

Serves: 2 to 4 people

Recipe Ingredients:

- 4 chicken breasts
- ½ cup of chicken broth /125ml
- 2 cups of green beans; cut in half /260g
- 2 cups of coconut milk /500ml
- 2 red bell pepper, seeded and cut in 2-inch sliced
- 2 yellow bell pepper, seeded and cut in 2-inch slices
- 4 tablespoons of red curry paste /60ml
- 2 tablespoons of lime juice /30ml
- 4 tablespoons of sugar /60g
- Salt and black pepper to taste

Cooking Instructions:

1. Add the chicken, red curry paste, salt, pepper, coconut milk, broth, and sugar, in the Foodi inner pot.

2. Close the pressure lid, secure the pressure valve, and select Pressure mode on High for about 15 minutes.

3. Press the Start/Stop button. Once the timer has ended, do a quick pressure release, and open the lid.

4. Remove the chicken onto a cutting board and close the crisping lid. Select the Broil function.

5. Add the bell peppers, green beans, and lime juice. Stir the sauce with a spoon and cook for about 4 minutes.

6. Slice the chicken with a knife, pour the sauce and vegetables over and serve warm.

Thyme Chicken with Veggies

Preparation time: 10 minutes

Cooking time: 30 minutes

Overall time: 40 minutes

Serves: 2 to 4 people

Recipe Ingredients:

- 4 skin-on, bone-in chicken legs
- ½ cup of dry white wine /125ml
- 1¼ cups of chicken stock /312.5ml
- 1 cup of carrots, thinly sliced /130g
- 1 cup of parsnip, thinly sliced /130g
- 4 slices of lemon
- 4 cloves of garlic; minced
- 3 tomatoes, thinly sliced
- 2 tablespoon of olive oil /30ml
- 1 tablespoon of honey /15ml
- 1 teaspoon of fresh chopped thyme /5g
- Salt and freshly ground black pepper to taste
- Fresh thyme; chopped for garnish

Cooking Instructions:

1. Season the chicken with pepper and salt. Warm oil on the Sear/Sauté function. Arrange chicken legs into the hot oil.

2. Cook for about 3 to 5 minutes each side until browned. Place in a bowl and set aside.

3. Cook thyme and garlic in the chicken fat for 1 minute until soft and lightly golden. Add wine into the pot to deglaze.

4. Scrape the pot's bottom to get rid of any brown bits of food. Simmer the wine for about 2 to 3 minutes until slightly reduced in volume.

5. Add stock, carrots, parsnips, tomatoes, pepper and salt into the pot. Lay reversible rack onto veggies. Into the Foodi's steamer basket, arrange chicken legs.

6. Set the steamer basket onto the reversible rack. Drizzle the chicken with honey then top with lemon slices.

7. Seal the pressure lid, choose Pressure, set to High, and set the timer to 12 minutes. Press the Start button.

8. Release the pressure naturally for about 10 minutes. Place the chicken onto a bowl. Drain the veggies and place them around the chicken.

9. Garnish with fresh thyme leaves before serving.

Whole Chicken with Lemon and Onion Stuffing

Preparation time: 15 minutes

Cooking time: 40 minutes

Overall time: 55 minutes

Serves: 2 to 4 people

Recipe Ingredients:

- 4 pounds of whole chicken
- 1 yellow onion, peeled and quartered
- 1 lemon, quartered
- 2 cloves of garlic, peeled
- 1 ¼ cups of chicken broth
- 1 tablespoon of herbes de Provence Seasoning
- 1 tablespoon of olive oil
- 1 teaspoon of garlic powder
- Salt and black pepper to season

Cooking Instructions:

1. Put the chicken on a clean flat surface and pat dry using paper towels.

2. Sprinkle the top and cavity of the chicken with salt, black pepper, Herbes de Provence, and garlic powder.

3. Stuff the onion, lemon quarters, and garlic cloves into the cavity. In the Foodi, fit the reversible rack. Pour the broth in and place the chicken on the rack.

4. Seal the lid, and select Pressure mode on High for about 25 minutes. Press the Start/Stop button to start cooking.

5. Once ready, do a natural pressure release for about 10 minutes, then a quick pressure release to let the remaining steam out, and press Stop.

6. Close the crisping lid and broil the chicken for about 5 minutes on Broil mode, to ensure that it attains a golden-brown color on each side.

7. Dish the chicken on a bed of steamed mixed veggies. Right here, the choice is yours to whip up some good veggies together as your appetite tells you.

Chicken with Crunchy Coconut Dumplings.

Preparation time: 10 minutes

Cooking time: 60 minutes

Overall time: 70 minutes

Serves: 2 to 4 people

Recipe Ingredients:

- 1 lb. of skinless, boneless chicken breasts; cubed
- 1 package of refrigerated biscuits, at room temperature
- ½ cup of heavy cream
- 2 cups of chicken stock
- 1 white onion; chopped
- 2 carrots; diced
- 2 celery stalks; diced
- 1 tablespoon of ghee
- 1 teaspoon of fresh rosemary
- ½ teaspoon of salt

Cooking Instructions:

1. Select the Sear/Sauté function on the pot and set to Medium High. Press the Start/Stop button to preheat the pot.

2. Melt the ghee and sauté the onion until softened, about 3 minutes. Pour the carrots, celery, chicken, and stock into the pot. Season with the rosemary and salt. Put the pressure lid together and lock in the Seal position.

3. Select Pressure, set to High, and set the time to 2 minutes. Press the Start/Stop button to begin.

4. When done cooking, perform a quick pressure release, and carefully open the lid. Stir the heavy cream into the soup.

5. Place the reversible rack in the higher position inside the pot, which will be over the soup and arrange the biscuits in a single layer in the rack.

6. Close the crisping lid. Select the Broil function and set the time to 15 minutes. Press the Start/Stop button to begin crisping. When ready, allow the biscuit and soup to rest for a few minutes and then serve.

Ground Turkey and Potato Chili

Preparation time: 15 minutes

Cooking time: 40 minutes

Overall time: 55 minutes

Serves: 2 to 4 people

Recipe Ingredients:

- 1 lb. of ground turkey /450g
- 2 bell peppers; chopped
- 6 potatoes, peeled and sliced
- 1 small onion; diced
- 2 garlic cloves; minced
- 1 cups of tomato puree /250ml
- 1 cup of diced tomatoes /130g
- 1 cup of chicken broth /250ml
- 1 cup of carrots; chopped /130g
- 1 cup of fresh or frozen corn kernels, roasted /130g
- 1 tablespoon of olive oil /15ml
- 1 tablespoon of ground cumin /15g
- 1 tablespoon of chili powder /15g
- Salt and fresh ground black pepper

Cooking Instructions:

1. Warm the olive on the Sear/Sauté function and stir-fry onions and garlic until soft, for about 3 minutes.

2. Press the start button and stir in turkey and cook until thoroughly browned, for about 6 minutes.

3. Add the remaining ingredients, and stir to combine. Seal the pressure lid, choose Pressure, set to High, and set the timer to 25 minutes; press the Start button.

4. When the time is up, do a quick pressure release. Set on the Sear/Sauté function. Cook uncovered for 15 more minutes. Serve warm.

Honey Garlic Chicken

Preparation time: 10 minutes

Cooking time: 20 minutes

Overall time: 30 minutes

Serves: 2 to 4 people

Recipe Ingredients:

- 4 boneless; skinless chicken breast; cut into chunks
- 4 garlic cloves, smashed
- 1 onion; diced
- ½ cup of honey
- 1 tablespoon of cornstarch
- 1 tablespoon of water
- 2 tablespoons of lime juice
- 3 tablespoons of soy sauce
- 2 teaspoon of sesame oil
- 1 teaspoon of rice vinegar
- Salt and black pepper to taste

Cooking Instructions:

1. Mix garlic, onion and chicken in your Foodi.

2. In a bowl, combine honey, sesame oil, lime juice, soy sauce, and rice vinegar; pour over the chicken mixture.

3. Seal the pressure lid, choose Pressure, set to High, and set the timer to 15 minutes, press the Start button.

4. When ready, release the pressure quickly. Mix water and cornstarch until well dissolved; stir into the sauce.

5. Press the Sear/Sauté function and simmer the sauce and cook for about 2 to 3 minutes as you stir until thickened.

Saucy Shredded Chicken

Preparation time: 10 minutes

Cooking time: 25 minutes

Overall time: 35 minutes

Serves: 2 to 4 people

Recipe Ingredients:

- 4 chicken breasts, skinless
- 2 cloves of garlic; minced
- ½ cup of chicken broth
- ¼ cup of Sriracha sauce
- ½ cup of honey
- 2 tablespoons of butter
- ½ teaspoon of red chili flakes
- 1 teaspoon of grated ginger
- ½ teaspoon of Cayenne pepper
- Salt and black pepper to taste
- Chopped scallion to garnish

Cooking Instructions:

1. In a bowl, pour the chicken broth. Mix in honey, ginger, sriracha sauce, red pepper flakes, cayenne pepper, and garlic, set it aside.

2. Put the chicken on a plate and season with salt and pepper. Set aside too. Select the Sear/Sauté function on High on your Foodi. Melt the butter, and add the chicken in 2 batches to brown on both sides for about 3 minutes.

3. Add the chicken back, and pour the pepper sauce over. Close the pressure lid, secure the pressure valve, and select Pressure mode on High for about 20 minutes.

4. Press the Start/Stop button. When ready, do a natural pressure release for about 5 minutes and open the lid.

5. Remove the chicken onto a cutting board and shred using two forks. Return the shredded chicken to the pot, close the crisping lid and Select the Air Crisp function.

6. Adjust the time to 4 minutes at 385 °F. When ready, transfer the chicken to a serving bowl, pour the sauce over. Garnish with the scallions. Serve with a side of sautéed mushrooms.

FISH AND SEAFOOD RECIPES

Potato Chowder with Peppery Prawns

Preparation time: 20 minutes

Cooking time: 60 minutes

Overall time: 80 minutes

Serves: 2 to 4 people

Recipe Ingredients:

- 4 slices of serrano ham; chopped
- 16 oz. of frozen corn
- 16 prawns, peeled and deveined
- 1 onion; chopped
- 2 Yukon Gold potatoes; chopped
- ¾ cup of heavy cream
- 2 cups of vegetable broth
- 2 tablespoons of olive oil
- 4 tablespoons of minced garlic; divided
- 1 teaspoon of dried rosemary
- 1 teaspoon of salt; divided
- 1 teaspoon of freshly ground black pepper; divided
- ½ teaspoon of red chili flakes

Cooking Instructions:

1. Select the Sear/Sauté function on the pot and set to Medium High. Press Start/Stop button to preheat the pot.

2. Add 1 tablespoon of the olive oil and cook the serrano ham, 2 tablespoons of garlic, and onion, stirring occasionally; for about 5 minutes.

3. Fetch out one-third of the serrano ham into a bowl for garnishing. Add the potatoes, corn, vegetable broth, rosemary, half of the salt, and half of the black pepper to the pot.

4. Seal the pressure lid, hit Pressure and set to High. Set the time to 10 minutes, and press the Start button.

5. In a bowl, toss the prawns in the remaining garlic, salt, black pepper, the remaining olive oil, and the red chili flakes.

6. When done cooking, do a quick pressure release and carefully open the pressure lid. Stir in the heavy cream and fix the reversible rack in the pot over the chowder.

7. Spread the prawn in the rack. Close the crisping lid. Select the Broil function and set the time to 8 minutes.

8. Press the Start/Stop button, when the timer has ended, remove the rack from the pot. Ladle the corn chowder into serving bowls and top with the prawns.

9. Garnish with the reserved ham and serve immediately.

Shrimp and Sausage Paella

Preparation time: 10 minutes

Cooking time: 1 hour

Overall time: 1 hour 10 minutes

Serves: 2 to 4 people

Recipe Ingredients:

- 1 lb. of andouille sausage; sliced
- 1 lb. of baby squid, cut into ¼-inch rings
- 1 lb. of jumbo shrimp, peeled and deveined
- 1 white onion; chopped
- 4 garlic cloves, minced
- 1 red bell pepper; diced
- 2 cups of Spanish rice
- 4 cups of chicken stock
- ½ cup of dry white wine
- 1 tablespoon of melted butter
- 1 teaspoon of turmeric powder
- 1½ teaspoons of sweet paprika
- ½ teaspoon of freshly ground black pepper
- ½ teaspoon of salt

Cooking Instructions:

1. Select the Sear/Sauté function on the pot and set to Medium High. Press the Start/Stop button to preheat the pot.

2. Melt the butter and add the sausage. Cook until browned on both sides, for about 3 minutes while stirring frequently.

3. Remove the sausage to a plate and set aside. Sauté the onion and garlic in the same fat for about 3 minutes until fragrant and pour in the wine.

4. Use a wooden spoon to scrape the bottom of the pot of any brown bits and cook for about 2 minutes or until the wine reduces by half.

5. Stir in the rice and water, season with the paprika, turmeric, black pepper, and salt. Seal the pressure lid, choose Pressure and set to High.

6. Set the time to 5 minutes, then press the Start/Stop button. When done cooking, do a quick pressure release and carefully open the lid.

7. Select the Sear/Sauté function, set to Medium High, and press the Start/Stop button. Add the squid and shrimp to the pot.

8. Stir gently without mashing the rice. Seal the pressure lid again and cook for about 6 minutes, until the shrimp are pink and opaque.

9. Return the sausage to the pot and mix in the bell pepper. Warm through for about 2 minutes. Dish the paella and serve immediately.

Scottish Seafood Curry

Preparation time: 10 minutes

Cooking time: 35 minutes

Overall time: 45 minutes

Serves: 2 to 4 people

Recipe Ingredients:

Seafood:

- ½ pound of squid, trimmed and cut into 1-inch rings
- ½ pound of Scallop meat
- ½ pound of mussel meat
- ½ pound of langoustine tall meat

Curry:

- 2 cups of shellfish stock
- 1 ½ cups of coconut milk
- 1 cup of milk
- 2 curry leaves
- 2 tablespoons of ginger paste
- 2 tablespoons of garlic paste
- 4 tablespoons of olive oil
- 2 tablespoons of Shallot puree
- 3 tablespoons of yellow curry paste
- 1 ½ tablespoons of chili powder
- 1 ½ tablespoons of chili paste
- 2 tablespoons of lemongrass paste
- 1 tablespoon of Grants Scotch Whiskey
- 2 tablespoons of fish curry powder
- 2 teaspoons of shrimp powder
- 1 teaspoon of shrimp paste
- ½ teaspoon of turmeric powder
- Salt to taste

Vegetables:

- ¼ cup of chopped okra
- ¼ cup of diced tomatoes
- ¼ cup of chopped onion
- ¼ cup of chopped eggplants

Cooking Instructions:

1. Add olive oil, shallot paste, yellow curry paste, ginger puree, garlic paste, lemongrass paste, chili paste, shrimp paste, and curry leaves.

2. Stir-fry for about 10 minutes on Sear/Sauté mode, until well combined and aromatic.

3. Add turmeric powder, fish curry powder, and shrimp powder. Stir-fry for 1 minute. Pour in the shellfish stock and close the crisping lid.

4. Cook on Broil mode for about 15 minutes. Open the lid, and add the scallops, squid; chopped onion, okra, tomatoes, and aubergine.

5. Stir lightly and close the pressure lid, secure the pressure valve, and select Steam mode on High pressure for about 5 minutes.

6. Press the Start/Stop button to start cooking. Once the timer has ended, do a quick pressure release, and open the lid.

7. Add milk, coconut milk, scotch whiskey, and salt. Stir carefully not to mash the aubergine. Select Sear/Sauté and add mussel meat and langoustine.

8. Stir carefully and simmer the sauce for about 3 minutes, press Stop, and turn off the Ninja Foodi. Dish the seafood with sauce and veggies into serving bowls.

9. Serve with a side of broccoli mash.

Mackerel en Papillote with Vegetables

Preparation time: 5 minutes

Cooking time: 20 minutes

Overall time: 25 minutes

Serves: 2 to 4 people

Recipe Ingredients:

- 3 large whole mackerel, cut into 2 pieces

- 1 lb. of asparagus, trimmed
- 1 carrot, cut into sticks
- 1 celery stalk, cut into sticks
- 3 cloves of garlic, minced
- 2 lemons, cut into wedges
- 6 medium tomatoes, quartered
- 1 large brown onion; sliced thinly
- 1 Orange Bell pepper, seeded and cut into sticks
- ½ cup of butter; at room temperature
- 1 ½ cups of water
- 2 ½ tablespoons of Pernod
- Salt and black pepper to taste

Cooking Instructions:

1. Cut out 6 pieces of parchment paper a little longer and wider than a piece of fish with kitchen scissors.

2. Cut out 6 pieces of foil slightly longer than the parchment papers. Lay the foil wraps on a flat surface and place each parchment paper on each aluminium foil.

3. In a bowl, add tomatoes, onions, garlic, bell pepper, pernod, butter, asparagus, carrot, celery, salt, and pepper. Use a spoon to mix them.

4. Place each fish piece on the layer of parchment and foil wraps. Spoon the vegetable mixture on each fish.

5. Wrap the fish and place the fish packets in the refrigerator to marinate for about 2 hours. Remove the fish to a flat surface.

6. Open the Ninja Foodi, pour the water in, and fit the reversible rack at the bottom of the pot. Put the packets on the trivet.

7. Seal the lid and select Steam mode on High pressure for about 3 minutes. Press the Start/Stop button to start cooking.

8. Once the timer has ended, do a quick pressure release, and open the lid. Remove the trivet with the fish packets onto a flat surface.

9. Carefully open the foil and using a spatula. Return the packets to the pot, on top of the rack.

10. Close the crisping lid and cook on Air Crisp function for about 3 minutes at 300°F. Then, remove to serving plates. Serve with lemon wedges.

Italian Flounder

Preparation time: 10 minutes

Cooking time: 1 hour

Overall time: 1 hour 10 minutes

Serves: 2 to 4 people

Recipe Ingredients:

- 4 flounder fillets
- 3 slices of prosciutto; chopped

- 2 (6 oz.) bags of baby kale
- ½ small red onion; chopped
- ½ cup of whipping cream
- 1 cup of panko breadcrumbs
- 2 tablespoons of chopped fresh parsley
- 3 tablespoons of unsalted butter, melted and divided
- ¼ teaspoon of fresh ground black pepper
- ½ teaspoon of salt; divided

Cooking Instructions:

1. Select the Sear/Sauté button on the Foodi and adjust to Medium. Press the Start button to preheat the inner pot.

2. Add the prosciutto and cook until crispy, for about 6 minutes. Stir in the red onions and cook for about 2 minutes or until the onions start to soften.

3. Sprinkle with half of the salt. Fetch the kale into the pot and cook, stirring frequently until wilted and most of the liquid has evaporated, for about 5 minutes.

4. Mix in the whipping cream. Lay the flounder fillets over the kale in a single layer. Brush 1 tablespoon of the melted butter over the fillets.

5. Sprinkle with the remaining salt and black pepper. Close the crisping lid and select the Bake/Roast function.

6. Adjust the temperature to 300°F and the cook time to 3 minutes. Press the Start button and combine the remaining butter, the parsley and breadcrumbs in a bowl.

7. When done cooking, open the crisping lid. Spoon the breadcrumbs mixture on the fillets. Close the crisping lid and select the Bake/Roast function.

8. Adjust the temperature to 400°F or 205°Cand the cook time to 6 minutes. Press the Start button.

9. After about 4 minutes, open the lid and check the fish. The breadcrumbs should be golden brown and crisp.

10. If not, close the lid and continue to cook for an additional two minutes.

Mussel Chowder with Oyster Crackers

Preparation time: 15 minutes

Cooking time: 1 hour

Overall time: 1 hour 15 minutes

Serves: 2 to 4 people

Recipe Ingredients:

- 1 lb. of parsnips, peeled and cut into chunks
- 3 (6 oz.) cans of chopped mussels, drained, liquid reserved

- 1½ cups of heavy cream
- 2 cups of oyster crackers
- ¼ cup of white wine
- ¼ cup of finely grated Pecorino Romano cheese
- 1 cup of clam juice
- 2 thick pancetta slices, cut into thirds
- 1 bay leaf
- 2 celery stalks; chopped
- 1 medium onion; chopped
- 1 tablespoon of flour
- 2 tablespoons of chopped fresh chervil
- 2 tablespoons of melted ghee
- ½ teaspoon of garlic powder
- 1 teaspoon of salt; divided
- 1 teaspoon of dried rosemary

Cooking Instructions:

1. Preheat the Foodi by close the crisping lid and Choose Air Crisp; adjust the temperature to 375°F and the time to 2 minutes and press the Start button.

2. In a bowl, pour in the oyster crackers. Drizzle with the melted ghee, add the cheese, garlic powder, and ½ teaspoon of salt.

3. Toss to coat the crackers and transfer to the crisping basket. Once the pot is ready, open the pressure lid and fix the basket in the pot.

4. Close the lid and select the Air Crisp function; adjust the temperature to 375°F and the cook time to 6 minutes and press the Start button.

5. After 3 minutes, carefully open the lid and mix the crackers with a spoon. Close the lid and resume cooking until crisp and lightly browned.

6. Take out the basket and set aside to cool. On the pot, select the Sear/Sauté button and adjust to Medium.

7. Press the start button and add the pancetta and cook for about 5 minutes, turning once or twice, until crispy.

8. Remove the pancetta to a paper towel-lined plate to drain fat and set it aside. Sauté the celery and onion in the pancetta grease for 1 minute until vegetables start softening.

9. Mix the flour into the vegetables to coat evenly and pour the wine over the veggies. Cook for about 1 minute or until reduced by about one-third.

10. Pour in the clam juice, the reserved mussel liquid, parsnips, remaining salt, rosemary, and bay leaf.

11. Seal the pressure lid, select the Pressure function adjust the pressure to High and the cook time to 4 minutes and press the Start button.

12. After cooking, perform a natural pressure release for about 5 minutes. Stir in the mussels and heavy cream.

13. Select the Sear/Sauté button and adjust to Medium. Press Start to simmer to the chowder and heat the mussels.

14. Carefully remove and discard the bay leaf after. Spoon the soup into bowls and crumble the pancetta over the top.

15. Garnish with the chervil and a handful of oyster crackers, serving the remaining crackers on the side.

Penne All Arrabbiata With Seafood and Chorizo

Preparation time: 10 minutes

Cooking time: 40 minutes

Overall time: 50 minutes

Serves: 2 to 4 people

Recipe Ingredients:

- 16 oz. of penne

- 8 oz. of shrimp, peeled and deveined
- 8 oz. of scallops
- 12 clams, cleaned and debearded
- 1 (24 oz.) jar of Arrabbiata sauce
- 1 onion; diced
- 3 cups of fish broth
- 1 chorizo; sliced
- 1 tablespoon of olive oil
- ½ teaspoon of freshly ground black pepper
- ½ teaspoon of salt

Cooking Instructions:

1. Select the Sear/Sauté button on the pot and set to Medium High. Select the Start/Stop button to preheat the pot.

2. Heat the oil and add the chorizo, onion, and garlic; sauté them for about 5 minutes. Stir in the penne, Arrabbiata sauce, and broth.

3. Season with the black pepper and salt and mix. Seal the pressure lid, choose Pressure, set to High and set the time to 2 minutes; press the Start button.

4. When the time is over, do a quick pressure release and carefully open the lid. Select the Sear/Sauté function and set to Medium High.

5. Press the Start/Stop button and stir in the shrimp, scallops, and clams. Put the pressure lid together and set to the Vent position.

6. Cover and cook for about 5 minutes, until the clams have opened and the shrimp and scallops are opaque and cooked through.

7. Discard any unopened clams. Spoon the seafood and chorizo pasta into serving bowls and serve warm.

Haddock with Sanfaina

Preparation time: 10 minutes

Cooking time: 30 minutes

Overall time: 40 minutes

Serves: 2 to 4 people

Recipe Ingredients:

- 4 haddock fillets

- 1 (14.5 oz.) can of diced tomatoes, drained
- ½ small onion; sliced
- 1 small jalapeño pepper, seeded and minced
- 2 large garlic cloves, minced
- 1 eggplant; cubed
- 1 bell pepper; chopped
- 1 bay leaf
- ⅓ cup of sliced green olives
- ¼ cup chopped fresh chervil; divided
- 3 tablespoons of olive oil
- 3 tablespoons of capers; divided
- ½ teaspoon of dried basil
- ¼ teaspoon of salt

Cooking Instructions:

1. Season the fish on both sides with salt, place in the refrigerator, and make the sauce. Select the Sear/Sauté function button and set to Medium.

2. Press the Start button and melt the butter until no longer foaming. Add onion, eggplant, bell pepper, jalapeño, and garlic; sauté for about 5 minutes.

3. Stir in the tomatoes, bay leaf, basil, olives, half of the chervil, and half of the capers. Remove the fish from the refrigerator and lay on the vegetables in the pot.

4. Seal the pressure lid, choose Pressure; adjust the pressure to Low and the cook time to 3 minutes and press the Start button.

5. After cooking, do a quick pressure release and carefully open the lid. Remove and discard the bay leaf.

6. Transfer the fish to a serving platter and spoon the sauce over. Sprinkle with the remaining chervil and capers. Serve.

Lemon Cod Goujons and Rosemary Chips

Preparation time: 10 minutes

Cooking time: 1 hour 30 minutes

Overall time: 1 hour 40 minutes

Serves: 2 to 4 people

Recipe Ingredients:

- 4 cod fillets, cut into strips

- 2 potatoes, cut into chips
- 4 lemon wedges to serve
- 2 eggs
- 1 cup of arrowroot starch
- 1 cup of flour
- 2 tablespoons of olive oil
- 3 tablespoons of fresh rosemary; chopped
- 1 tablespoon of cumin powder
- ½ tablespoon of cayenne powder
- 1 teaspoon of black pepper, plus more for seasoning
- 1 teaspoon of salt, plus more for seasoning
- Zest and juice from 1 lemon
- Cooking spray

Cooking Instructions:

1. Fix the Crisping Basket in the pot and close the crisping lid. Select the Air Crisp function and set the temperature to 375°F, and the time to 5 minutes.

2. Press the Start/Stop button to preheat the pot. In a bowl, whisk the eggs, lemon zest, and lemon juice.

3. In another bowl, combine the arrowroot starch, flour, cayenne powder, cumin, black pepper, and salt.

4. Coat each cod strip in the egg mixture, and then dredge in the flour mixture, coating well on all sides. Grease the preheated basket with cooking spray.

5. Place the coated fish in the basket and oil with cooking spray. Close the crisping lid and select the Air Crisp function.

6. Set the temperature to 375°F, and the time to 15 minutes; press the Start/Stop button. Toss the potatoes with oil and season with salt and pepper.

7. After 15 minutes, check the fish making sure the pieces are as crispy as desired. Remove the fish from the basket. Pour the potatoes in the basket.

8. Close the crisping lid; choose Air Crisp, set the temperature to 400°F, and the time to 24 minutes; press the Start/Stop button.

9. After 12 minutes, open the lid, remove the basket and shake the fries. Return the basket to the pot and close the lid to continue cooking until crispy.

10. When ready, sprinkle with fresh rosemary. Serve the fish with the potatoes and lemon wedges.

Salmon with Creamy Grits

Preparation time: 10 minutes

Cooking time: 1 hour 30 minutes

Overall time: 1 hour 490 minutes

Serves: 2 to 4 people

Recipe Ingredients:

- 4 salmon fillets, skin removed

- 1½ cups of vegetable stock
- ¾ cup of corn grits
- ½ cups of coconut milk
- 3 tablespoons of Cajun
- 1 tablespoon of packed brown sugar/
- 3 tablespoons of butter; divided
- 2 teaspoons of salt
- Cooking spray

Cooking Instructions:

1. Pour the grits into a heatproof bowl. Add the coconut milk, stock, 1 tablespoon of butter, and ½ teaspoon of salt.

2. Stir and cover the bowl with foil. Pour the water into the inner pot. Put the reversible rack in the pot and place the bowl on top.

3. Seal the pressure lid, select the Pressure function; adjust the pressure to High and the cook time to 15 minutes.

4. Press the Start button to begin cooking. In a bowl combine the Cajun, brown sugar, and remaining salt.

5. Oil the fillets on one side with cooking spray and place one or two at a time with sprayed-side down into the spice mixture.

6. Oil the other sides and turn over to coat that side in the seasoning. Repeat the process with the remaining fillets.

7. Once the grits are ready, perform a natural pressure release for about 10 minutes. Remove the rack and bowl from the pot.

8. Add the remaining butter to the grits and stir to combine well. Cover again with aluminum foil and return the bowl to the pot (without the rack).

9. Fix the rack in the upper position of the pot and put the salmon fillets on the rack. Close the crisping lid and select the Bake/Roast function.

10. Adjust the temperature to 400°F and the cook time to 12 minutes. Press the Start button. After 6 minutes, open the lid and use tongs to turn the fillets over.

11. Close the lid and continue cooking. When the salmon is ready, take out the rack. Remove the bowl of grits and take off the foil.

12. Stir and serve immediately with the salmon.

Creamy Crab Soup

Preparation 10 minutes

Cooking time: 35 minutes

Overall time: 45 minutes

Serves: 2 to 4 people

Recipe Ingredients:

- 2 pounds of Crabmeat Lumps
- 2 celery stalk; diced

- 1 white onion; chopped
- ¾ cup of heavy cream
- ½ cup of Half and Half cream
- 1 ½ cup of chicken broth
- ¾ cup of Muscadet
- 6 tablespoons of butter
- 6 tablespoons of flour
- 3 teaspoons of Worcestershire sauce
- 3 teaspoons of old bay Seasoning
- 2 teaspoons of Hot sauce
- 3 teaspoons of minced garlic
- Salt to taste
- Lemon juice to serve
- Chopped dill to serve

Cooking Instructions:

1. Melt the butter on Sear/Sauté mode, and mix in the all-purpose flour, in a fast motion to make a rue.

2. Add celery, onion, and garlic. Stir and cook until soft and crispy; for about 3 minutes.

3. While stirring, gradually add the half and half cream, heavy cream, and broth. Let simmer for about 2 minutes.

4. Add Worcestershire sauce, old bay seasoning, Muscadet, and hot sauce. Stir and let simmer for about 15 minutes.

5. Add the crabmeat and mix it well into the sauce. Close the crisping lid and cook on Broil mode for 10 minutes to soften the meat.

6. Dish into serving bowls, garnish with dill and drizzle squirts of lemon juice over. Serve with a side of garlic crusted bread.

Parmesan Tilapia

Preparation time: 5 minutes

Cooking time: 10 minutes

Overall time: 15 minutes

Serves: 2 to 4 people

Recipe Ingredients:

- ¾ cup of grated Parmesan cheese
- 4 tilapia fillets

- 1 tablespoon of olive oil
- 1 tablespoon of chopped parsley
- ¼ teaspoon of garlic powder
- 2 teaspoons of paprika
- ¼ teaspoon of salt

Cooking Instructions:

1. Mix parsley, Parmesan, garlic, salt, and paprika, in a shallow bowl.

2. Brush the olive oil over the fillets, and then coat them with the Parmesan mixture. Place the tilapia onto a lined baking sheet, and then into the Ninja Foodi.

3. Close the crisping lid and cook for about 5 minutes on all sides on Air Crisp mode at 350°F.

Fried Salmon

Preparation time: 5 minutes

Cooking time: 10 minutes

Overall time: 15 minutes

Serves: 1 to 3 people

Recipe Ingredients:

- 1 salmon fillet.
- ¼ teaspoon of garlic powder

- 1 tablespoon of soy sauce
- Salt and pepper

Cooking Instructions:

1. Combine the soy sauce with the garlic powder, salt, and pepper.

2. Brush the mixture over the salmon. Place the salmon onto a sheet of parchment paper and inside the Ninja Foodi.

3. Close the crisping lid and cook for about 10 minutes on Air Crisp at 350°F, until crispy on the outside and tender on the inside.

Cajun Salmon with Lemon

Preparation time: 5 minutes

Cooking time: 5 minutes

Overall time: 10 minutes

Serves: 1 to 3 people

Recipe Ingredients:

- 1 salmon fillet
- Juice of ½ lemon

- 2 lemon wedges
- 1 tablespoon of Cajun seasoning
- 1 tablespoon of chopped parsley; for garnishing
- ¼ teaspoon of brown sugar

Cooking Instructions:

1. Combine the sugar and lemon and coat the salmon with this mixture thoroughly. Coat the salmon with the Cajun seasoning as well.

2. Place a parchment paper into the Ninja Foodi, close the crisping lid and cook the salmon for about 7 minutes on Air Crisp mode at 350°F.

3. If you use a thicker fillet, cook no more than 6 minutes. Serve with lemon wedges and chopped parsley.

Cod Cornflakes Nuggets

Preparation time: 5 minutes

Cooking time: 20 minutes

Overall time: 25 minutes

Serves: 2 to 4 people

Recipe Ingredients:

- 1 ¼ pounds of cod fillets, cut into chunks
- 1 egg

- 1 cup of cornflakes
- ½ cup of flour
- 1 tablespoon of olive oil
- 1 tablespoon of water
- Salt and pepper, to taste

Cooking Instructions:

1. Add the oil and cornflakes in a food processor, and process until crumbed.

2. Season the fish chunks with salt and pepper. Beat the egg along with 1 tablespoon of water.

3. Dredge the chunks in flour first, then dip in the egg, and coat with cornflakes. Arrange on a lined sheet.

4. Close the crisping lid and cook at 350°F for about 15 minutes on Air Crisp mode. Serve immediately and enjoy!

BEEF, PORK AND LAMB RECIPES

Peanut Sauce Beef Satay

Preparation time: 10 minutes

Cooking time: 50 minutes

Overall time: 1 hour

Serves: 2 to 4 people

Recipe Ingredients:

- 1 lb. of flank steak

- 1 tablespoon of coconut aminos
- 1 tablespoon of lime juice
- 1 tablespoon of coconut oil
- 1½ teaspoons of red curry paste
- ½ teaspoon of salt

For the Cucumber Relish:

- 1 serrano chile; cut into thin rounds
- ½ cucumber
- ½ cup of rice vinegar
- ¼ cup of water
- 2 tablespoons of sugar
- 1 teaspoon of salt

For the Sauce:

- 1 cup of coconut milk
- ½ cup of peanut butter
- ⅓ cup of water
- 1 tablespoon of lime juice
- 1 tablespoon of onion; minced
- 1 tablespoon of coconut oil
- 1 teaspoon of garlic; minced
- 2 teaspoons of red curry paste
- 1 teaspoon of brown sugar

Cooking Instructions:

1. Season both sides of the steak with salt. Put in a resealable plastic bag, set it aside, and make the marinade.

2. In a small bowl, whisk the lime juice, curry paste, coconut aminos, and coconut oil. Pour the marinade over the steak, seal the bag

3. Massage the bag to coat the meat. Set it aside for about 20 minutes. While the steak marinates; cut the cucumber into ¼-inch slices, then into quarters.

4. In a bowl, whisk the vinegar, water, sugar, and salt until the sugar and salt dissolve. Add the cucumber pieces, refrigerate until needed.

5. On the Foodi, select the Sear/Sauté function and adjust to Medium-High. Press the Start button to preheat the pot for about 5 minutes.

6. Heat the coconut oil until shimmering and sauté the onion and garlic in the pot. Cook for about 1 to 2 minutes or until fragrant.

7. Stir in the coconut milk, curry paste, and brown sugar. Seal the pressure lid, choose Pressure; adjust the pressure to High and the cook time to 0 minutes.

8. Press the Start button. After cooking, perform a quick pressure release, and carefully open the lid. Pour in the water and mix.

9. Remove the meat from the marinade, holding the meat above the bag for a while to drain the excess marinade, put on the reversible rack.

10. Put the rack with the steak in the upper position of the pot above the sauce. Close the crisping lid; select the Broil function.

11. Adjust the cook time to 14 minutes, and press Start to begin cooking. After about 7 minutes, open the lid and turn the steak.

12. Close the lid and begin broiling. Transfer the steak to a cutting board and allow resting for a few minutes.

13. While the steak cools, mix the peanut butter and lime juice into the sauce. Taste and adjust the seasoning.

14. Cut the steak into thin slices and serve with the peanut sauce and cucumber relish.

Beef Carnitas

Preparation time: 5 minutes

Cooking time: 50 minutes

Overall time: 55 minutes

Serves: 2 to 4 people

Recipe Ingredients:

- 2½ lb. of bone-in country ribs
- 1 small onion; cut into 8 wedges
- 3 garlic cloves, smashed and peeled

- ¼ cup of orange juice
- 2 tablespoons of beef stock
- 1 tablespoon of lime juice
- 1 teaspoon of salt
- Cooking spray

Cooking Instructions:

1. Season the ribs with salt on all sides. In the Foodi's inner pot, combine the orange juice, stock, and lime juice.

2. Drop in the onion and garlic; stir. Put the ribs in the pot, Seal the pressure lid, select the Pressure function.

3. Adjust the pressure to High and the cook time to 25 minutes. Press the Start/Stop button to begin cooking.

4. After cooking, do a natural pressure release for about 12 minutes. Transfer the ribs to a plate to cool slightly.

5. Remove and discard the bones, run the juice in the pot through a fat separator and set aside for a few minutes.

6. Pour the sauce back into the pot and reserve the fat. Close the crisping lid and select the Air Crisp function.

7. Adjust the temperature to 400°F and the time to 3 minutes to preheat; press the Start button.

8. Oil the reversible rack with cooking spray and lay the ribs in a single layer on the rack. Baste with the reserved fat.

9. When the Foodi is heated, put the rack in the pot in the upper position. Close the crisping lid and select the Air Crisp function;

10. Adjust the temperature to 375°F and the cook time to 6 minutes; press the Start button.

11. After crisping, put the beef back in the sauce and use long forks to shred the meat. Stir the beef into the sauce.

12. Serve the carnitas with flat bread or on rice.

Cheese Burgers in Hoagies

Preparation time: 15 minutes

Cooking time: 50 minutes

Overall time: 1 hour 5 minutes

Serves: 2 to 4 people

Recipe Ingredients:

- 1 lb. chuck beef roast
- 1 (14 oz) can French onion soup

- 3 slices of Provolone cheese
- 3 hoagies, halved
- 1 onion; sliced
- 2 cups of beef broth
- 1 tablespoon of olive oil
- 2 tablespoons of Worcestershire sauce
- 1 teaspoon of garlic powder
- 3 teaspoons of mayonnaise
- Salt and black pepper to taste

Cooking Instructions:

1. Season the beef with garlic powder, salt, and pepper. On your Foodi, select the Sear/Sauté function. Heat the olive oil and brown the beef on both sides for about 5 minutes.

2. Remove the meat onto a plate. Into the pot, add the onions and cook until soft. Then, pour the beef broth and stir, while scraping the bottom off every stuck bit.

3. Add the onion soup, Worcestershire sauce, and beef. Close the lid, secure the pressure valve, and select Pressure mode on High pressure for about 20 minutes.

4. Press the Start/Stop button. Once the timer has stopped, do a natural pressure release for about 15 minutes. Do a quick pressure release to let out any remaining steam. Use two forks to shred the meat.

5. Close the crisping lid and cook on the Bake/Roast function for about 10 minutes at 350 °F, open the lid and strain the juice of the pot through a sieve into a bowl.

6. Assemble the burgers by slathering mayo on halved hoagies, spoon the shredded meat over and top each hoagie with cheese.

Beef and Pepperoncini Peppers

Preparation time: 10 minutes

Cooking time: 25 minutes

Overall time: 55 minutes

Serves: 2 to 4 people

Recipe Ingredients:

- 2 pounds of beef roast; cut into cubes
- 1 pack of brown gravy mix

- 1 pack of Italian salad dressing mix
- 14 ounces of jar pepperoncini peppers, with liquid
- ½ cup of water

Cooking Instructions:

1. Place the beef, pepperoncini peppers, brown gravy mix, Italian salad dressing mix, and water, in Foodi's inner pot.

2. Close the lid, secure the pressure valve, and select Pressure function on High pressure mode for about 35 minutes.

3. Press the Start/Stop button to start cooking. Once the timer has stopped, do a quick pressure release, and open the pot.

4. Close the crisping lid and cook on Bake/Roast function for 20 minutes at 380°F, until nice and tender.

5. When ready, dish the ingredients into a bowl and use two forks to shred the beef. Serve beef sauce in plates with a side of a veggie mash, or bread.

Red Pork and Chickpea Stew

Preparation time: 10 minutes

Cooking time: 30 minutes

Overall time: 40 minutes

Serves: 2 to 4 people

Recipe Ingredients:

- 1 (3 lb.) boneless pork shoulder, trimmed and cubed
- 15 oz. of canned chickpeas, drained and rinsed

- 1½ cups of water
- ½ cup of sweet paprika
- 1 bay leaf
- 2 red bell peppers; chopped
- 6 cloves of garlic; minced
- 1 white onion; chopped
- 1 tablespoon of cornstarch
- 1 tablespoon of olive oil
- 1 tablespoon of chilli powder
- 1 tablespoon of water
- 2 teaspoons of salt

Cooking Instructions:

1. Select the Sear/Sauté function and set to Medium High, press the Start/Stop button to preheat the pot.

2. Add pork and oil and allow cooking for about 5 minutes until browned. Add in the onion, paprika, bay leaf, salt, water, chickpeas, and chili powder.

3. Seal the pressure lid, choose Pressure, set to High, and set the timer to 8 minutes and press the Start button.

4. When the time is up, Do a quick release and discard bay leaf. Remove 1 cup of cooking liquid from the Foodi.

5. Add to a blender alongside garlic, water, cornstarch, and red bell peppers; blend well until smooth. Add the blended mixture into the stew and mix well.

Chorizo Stuffed Yellow Bell Peppers

Preparation time: 10 minutes

Cooking time: 30 minutes

Overall time: 40 minutes

Serves: 2 to 4 people

Recipe Ingredients:

- ¾ lb. of chorizo

- 1 small onion; diced
- ⅔ cup of diced fresh tomatoes
- 1½ cups of cooked rice
- 1 cup of shredded Mexican blend cheese; divided
- 4 large yellow bell peppers
- 2 teaspoons of olive oil

Cooking Instructions:

1. Cut about ¼ to ⅓ inch off the top of each pepper. Cut through the ribs inside the peppers and pull out the core and remove as much of the ribs as possible.

2. On the Foodi, select the Sear/Sauté function and adjust to Medium. Press the Start button to preheat the inner pot for about 5 minutes.

3. Heat the oil in the pot until shimmering and cook in the chorizo while breaking the meat with a spatula.

4. Cook until just starting to brown, for about 2 minutes. Add the onion and sauté until the vegetables soften and the chorizo has now browned, about 3 minutes.

5. Turn the Foodi off and scoop the chorizo and vegetables into a medium bowl. Add the tomatoes, rice, and ½ cup of cheese to the bowl.

6. Mix to combine well. Spoon the filling mixture into the bell peppers to the brim. Clean the inner pot with a paper towel and return the pot to the base.

7. Pour 1 cup of water into the pot and fix the rack in the pot in the lower position. Put the peppers on the rack and cover the tops loosely with a piece of foil.

8. Lock the pressure lid into place and set to Seal. Select the Pressure function and adjust the pressure to High and the time to 12 minutes and press the Start.

9. After cooking, perform a quick pressure release and carefully open the lid. Remove the foil from the top of the peppers.

10. Sprinkle the remaining ½ cup of cheese on the peppers. Close the crisping lid; select the Broil function, adjust the time to 5 minutes.

11. Press the Start button to broil the cheese. After 4 minutes, open the lid and check the peppers.

12. The cheese should have melted and browned a bit. If not, close the lid and continue cooking. Let the peppers cool for several minutes before serving.

Beef Soup with Tortillas

Preparation time: 10 minutes

Cooking time: 20 minutes

Overall time: 30 minutes

Serves: 2 to 4 people

Recipe Ingredients:

- 3 pounds of ground beef, grass fed
- 2 medium yellow onion; chopped

- 6 green bell pepper, diced
- 6 cups of chopped tomatoes
- ½ cup of chopped green chilies
- 3 cups of bone broth
- 3 cups of milk
- 2 tablespoons of cumin powder
- 2 tablespoons of olive oil
- 3 tablespoons of chili powder
- 1 teaspoon of cinnamon
- 1 teaspoon of onion powder
- 2 teaspoons of paprika
- 1 teaspoon of garlic powder
- Salt and black pepper to taste

Topping:

- Chopped Jalapenos, cilantro and green onions; sliced Avocados, lime juice

Cooking Instructions:

1. Select the Sear/Sauté function and set High on your Foodi. Pour in the oil, once it has heated, add the yellow onion and green peppers.

2. Sauté until they are soft for about 5 minutes. Include the ground beef, stir the ingredients, and let the beef cook for about 8 minutes until it browns.

3. Next, add the chili powder, cumin powder, black pepper, paprika, cinnamon, garlic powder, onion powder, and green chilies. Give them a good stir.

4. Top with tomatoes, milk, and bone broth. Close the lid, secure the pressure valve, and select Pressure mode on High for about 20 minutes.

5. Press the Start button. Once the timer has ended, do a quick pressure release. Adjust the taste with salt and pepper.

6. Dish the taco soup into serving bowls and add the toppings. Serve warm with a side of tortillas.

Honey Short Ribs with Rosemary Potatoes

Preparation time: 20 minutes

Cooking time: 1 hour 25 minutes

Overall time: 1 hour 45 minutes

Serves: 2 to 4 people

Recipe Ingredients:

- 4 bone-in beef short ribs, silver skin
- 2 potatoes, peeled and cut into 1-inch pieces
- ½ cup of beef broth

- 3 garlic cloves; minced
- 1 onion; chopped
- 2 tablespoons of olive oil
- 2 tablespoons of honey
- 2 tablespoons of minced fresh rosemary
- 1 teaspoon of salt
- 1 teaspoon of black pepper

Cooking Instructions:

1. Select the Sear/Sauté function on the pot and set to High. Press the Start/Stop button to preheat the pot.

2. Season the short ribs on all sides with ½ teaspoon of salt and ½ teaspoon of pepper.

3. Heat 1 tbsp of olive oil and brown the ribs on all sides, for about 10 minutes total. Stir in the onion, honey, broth, 1 tbsp of rosemary, and garlic.

4. Seal the pressure lid, choose Pressure, set to High, and set the time to 40 minutes. Select the Start/Stop button to begin.

5. In a large bowl, toss the potatoes with the remaining oil, rosemary, salt, and black pepper.

6. When the ribs are ready, perform a quick pressure release and carefully open the lid. Fix the reversible rack in the higher position of the pot, which is over the ribs.

7. Put the potatoes on the rack. Close the crisping lid. Select the Bake/Roast function, set the temperature to 350°F, and set the time to 15 minutes.

8. Press the Start/Stop button to begin roasting. Once the potatoes are tender and roasted, use tongs to pick the potatoes and the short ribs into a plate; set aside.

9. Select the Sear/Sauté function and set to High. Simmer the sauce for about 5 minutes and spoon the sauce into a bowl.

10. Allow sitting for 2 minutes and scoop off the fat that forms on top. Serve the ribs with the potatoes and sauce.

Calzones with Sausage and Mozzarella

Preparation time: 10 minutes

Cooking time: 25 minutes

Overall time: 35 minutes

Serves: 2 to 4 people

Recipe Ingredients:

- 1 lb. of pound frozen bread dough
- 1 small green bell pepper, seeded and chopped
- 3 Italian sausages

- ¼ cup of tomato sauce
- 1 cup of shredded mozzarella cheese
- 2 tablespoons of olive oil

Cooking Instructions:

1. On your Foodi, select the Sear/Sauté function and adjust to Medium-High to preheat the inner pot.

2. Press the Start button to preheat the pot. Heat 1 tbsp of olive oil in the pot and sauté the bell pepper for 1 minute or until just starting to soften.

3. Remove the pepper into a plate and set aside. Brown the sausages for about 3 minutes on one side. Turn the sausages and brown the other side.

4. Add ¾ cup of water to the inner pot. Lock the pressure lid into place and set to seal. Choose Pressure; adjust the pressure to High and the cook time to 4 minutes.

5. Press the Start button. After cooking, perform a quick pressure release and carefully open the pressure lid.

6. Remove the sausages from the pot onto a cutting board and cool it for some minutes.

7. Discard the water in the pot, wipe the pot dry with a clean napkin, and return the pot to the base. When the sausages have cooled, slice into ¼-inch rounds.

8. Cut four pieces of parchment paper about 8 inches and divide the dough into four equal pieces.

9. One at a time and on a piece of parchment, use your hands to press each dough into a circle about 6 to 7 inches in diameter.

10. Lose the crisping lid, select the Bake/Roast and adjust the temperature to 400°F. Press Start to preheat the pot for about 5 minutes.

11. While the preheats, make the calzones. One after the other, spread 1 tablespoon of tomato sauce over half a dough circle, leaving a ½-inch clear border.

12. Arrange the sausage rounds in a single layer and sprinkle a quarter of the green peppers over the top.

13. Top with a quarter cup of cheese. Use the parchment to pull the other side of the dough over the filling and pinch the edges together to seal.

14. Repeat the process with another dough. Cut the parchment around each calzone, so it is about ½ inch larger than the calzone.

15. Brush the calzones with some of the remaining olive oil. With a large spatula, transfer the two calzones to the reversible rack set in the lower position in the pot.

16. Open the lid and place the rack in the pot. Close the crisping lid and select the Bake/Roast function/

17. Adjust the temperature to 400°F and the cook time to 12 minutes. Press the Start button. After 6 minutes, check the calzones, which will be a dark golden brown.

18. Remove the rack and turn the calzones over. Remove the parchment paper and brush the tops with a little olive oil. Return the rack to the pot.

19. Close the lid and continue cooking for the last 6 minutes. While the first two calzones bake, assemble the remaining two.

20. When the first set of calzones are done, transfer to a wire rack to cool and bake the second batch.

Chunky Pork Meatloaf with Mashed Potatoes

Preparation time: 15 minutes

Cooking time: 40 minutes

Overall time: 55 minutes

Serves: 2 to 4 people

Recipe Ingredients:

- 2 lb. of potatoes; cut into large chunks
- 12 oz. of pork meatloaf

- 2 garlic cloves; minced
- 2 large eggs
- 12 individual saltine crackers, crushed
- 1¾ cups of full cream milk; divided
- 1 cup of chopped white onion
- ½ cup of heavy cream
- ¼ cup of barbecue sauce
- 1 tablespoon of olive oil
- 3 tablespoons of chopped fresh cilantro
- 3 tablespoons of unsalted butter
- ¼ teaspoon of dried rosemary
- 1 teaspoon of yellow mustard
- 1 teaspoon of Worcestershire sauce
- 2 teaspoons of salt
- ½ teaspoon of black pepper

Cooking Instructions:

1. Select the Sear/Sauté function and adjust to Medium.

2. Press the Start button to preheat the pot for about 5 minutes. Heat the olive oil until shimmering and sauté the onion and garlic in the oil.

3. Cook for about 2 minutes until the onion softens. Transfer the onion and garlic to a plate and set aside.

4. In a bowl, crumble the meatloaf mix into small pieces. Sprinkle with 1 teaspoon of salt, the pepper, cilantro, and thyme. Add the sautéed onion and garlic.

5. Sprinkle the crushed saltine crackers over the meat and seasonings. In a small bowl, beat ¼ cup of milk, the eggs, mustard, and Worcestershire sauce.

6. Pour the mixture on the layered cracker crumbs and gently mix the ingredients in the bowl with your hands. Shape the meat mixture into an 8-inch round.

7. Cover the reversible rack with aluminum foil and carefully lift the meatloaf into the rack. Pour the remaining 1½ cups of milk and the heavy cream into the inner pot.

8. Add the potatoes, butter, and remaining salt. Place the rack with meatloaf over the potatoes in the upper position in the pot.

9. Seal the pressure lid, select the Pressure function and adjust the pressure to High and the cook time to 25 minutes.

10. Press the Start button. When the cooking time is up, perform a quick pressure release, and carefully open the pressure lid.

11. Brush the meatloaf with the barbecue sauce. Close the crisping lid; choose Broil and adjust the cook time to 7 minutes.

12. Press the Start button to begin grilling. When the top has browned, remove the rack, and transfer the meatloaf to a serving platter.

13. Mash the potatoes in the pot. Slice the meatloaf and serve with the mashed potatoes.

Beef Stew with Beer

Preparation time: 10 minutes

Cooking time: 50 minutes

Overall time: 1 hour

Serves: 2 to 4 people

Recipe Ingredients:

- 2 lb. beef stewed meat; cut into bite-size pieces
- 1 packet dry onion soup mix

- 2 cloves garlic; minced
- 2 cups beef broth
- ¼ cup flour
- 1 medium bottle beer
- 3 tbsp butter
- 2 tbsp Worcestershire sauce
- 1 tbsp tomato paste
- Salt and black pepper to taste

Cooking Instructions:

1. In a zipper bag, add beef, salt, all-purpose flour, and pepper. Close the bag up and shake it to coat the meat well with the mixture.

2. Select the Sear/Sauté function on the Foodi. Melt the butter, and brown the beef on both sides, for about 5 minutes.

3. Pour the broth to deglaze the bottom of the pot. Stir in tomato paste, beer, Worcestershire sauce, and the onion soup mix.

4. Close the lid, secure the pressure valve, and select the Pressure function on High pressure for about 25 minutes.

5. Press the Start/Stop button to start cooking. Once the timer is done, do a natural pressure release for about 10 minutes.

6. Then do a quick pressure release to let out any remaining steam. Open the pressure lid and close the crisping lid.

7. Cook on the Broil function for 10 minutes. Spoon the beef stew into serving bowls and serve with over a bed of vegetable mash with steamed greens.

Braised Short Ribs wituh Mushrooms

Preparation time: 10 minutes

Cooking time: 50 minutes

Overall time: 1 hour

Serves: 2 to 4 people

Recipe Ingredients:

- 2 lb. of beef short ribs
- 1 small onion; sliced

- 1 bell pepper; diced
- 4 garlic cloves, smashed o
- ⅓ cup of beef broth
- 1 cup of beer
- 1 cup of crimini mushrooms; sliced
- 1 tablespoon of olive oil
- 1 tablespoon of soy sauce
- 1 teaspoon of smoked paprika
- ½ teaspoon of dried oregano
- ½ teaspoon of cayenne pepper
- Salt and ground black pepper to taste

Cooking Instructions:

1. In a small bowl, combine pepper, paprika, cayenne pepper, salt, and oregano. Rub the seasoning mixture on all sides of the short ribs.

2. Warm oil on the Sear/Sauté function. Add mushrooms and cook until browned, for about 8 minutes; set aside.

3. Add short ribs to the Foodi, and cook for about 3 minutes for each side until browned; set aside on a plate.

4. Throw in garlic and onion to the oil and stir-fry for about 2 minutes until fragrant. Add in beer to deglaze.

5. Scrape the pot's bottom to get rid of any browned bits of food; bring to a simmer and cook for about 2 minutes until reduced slightly.

6. Stir in soy sauce, bell pepper and beef broth. Dip short ribs into the liquid in a single layer.

7. Seal the pressure lid, choose Pressure, set to High, and set the timer to 40 minutes. Press the Start button.

8. Release pressure naturally for about 10 minutes. Divide the ribs with the sauce into bowls and top with fried mushrooms.

Beef and Broccoli Sauce

Preparation time: 10 minutes

Cooking time: 25 minutes

Overall time: 35 minutes

Serves: 2 to 4 people

Recipe Ingredients:

- 2 pounds of chuck roast, boneless and cut into thin strips
- 4 cloves of garlic; minced

- 1 cup beef broth
- ¾ cup of soy sauce
- 7 cups of broccoli florets
- 1 tablespoon of cornstarch
- 1 tablespoon of olive oil
- Salt to taste

Cooking Instructions:

1. Open the lid of Foodi, and select the Sear/Sauté function. Add the olive oil, and once heated, add the beef and minced garlic.

2. Cook the meat until brown. Stir in soy sauce and beef broth. Close the lid, secure the pressure valve, and select Pressure mode on High pressure for about 10 minutes.

3. Press the Start/Stop button to start cooking. Once the timer has ended, do a quick pressure release and remove the meat and set aside.

4. Use a soup spoon to fetch out a quarter of the liquid into a bowl, add the cornstarch, and mix it until it is well dissolved.

5. Pour the starch mixture into the pot and place the reversible rack. Place the broccoli florets on it and seal the pressure lid.

6. Select the Steam function on LOW mode for about 5 minutes. When ready, do a quick pressure release and open the lid.

7. Remove the rack, stir the sauce, add the meat and close the crisping lid. Cook for about 5 minutes on the Broil function.

8. The sauce should be thick enough when you finish cooking. Dish the beef broccoli sauce into a serving bowl and serve with a side of cooked pasta.

Short Ribs with Egg Noodles

Preparation time: 15 minutes

Cooking time: 50 minutes

Overall time: 1 hour 5 minutes

Serves: 2 to 4 people

Recipe Ingredients:

- 4 lb. of bone-in short ribs

- 1 garlic clove; minced
- 1½ cups of panko bread crumbs
- Low-sodium beef broth
- 6 oz. of egg noodles
- 3 tablespoons of melted unsalted butter
- 2 tablespoons of prepared horseradish
- 6 tablespoons of Dijon mustard
- 2½ teaspoon of salt
- ½ teaspoon of freshly ground black pepper

Cooking Instructions:

1. Season the short ribs on all sides with 1½ teaspoons of salt. Pour 1 cup of broth into the inner pot.

2. Put the reversible rack in the lower position in the pot, and place the short ribs on top.

3. Seal the pressure lid, choose Pressure; adjust the pressure to High and the time to 25 minutes; press the Start button.

4. After cooking, perform a natural pressure release for about 5 minutes, then a quick pressure release, and carefully open the lid.

5. Remove the rack and short ribs. Pour the cooking liquid into a measuring cup to get 2 cups. If lesser than 2 cups, add more broth and season with salt and pepper.

6. Add the egg noodles and the remaining salt. Stir and submerge the noodles as much as possible.

7. Seal the pressure lid, choose Pressure; adjust the pressure to High and the cook time to 4 minutes; press Start.

8. In a bowl, combine the horseradish, Dijon mustard, garlic, and black pepper. Brush the sauce on all sides of the short ribs and reserve any extra sauce.

9. In a bowl, mix the butter and breadcrumbs. Coat the ribs with the crumbs. Put the ribs back on the rack.

10. After cooking, do a quick pressure release, and carefully open the lid. Stir the noodles, which may not be quite done but will continue cooking.

11. Return the rack and beef to the pot in the upper position. Close the crisping lid and select the Bake/Roast function.

12. Adjust the temperature to 400°F or 205°C and the cook time to 15 minutes. Press the Start button.

13. After 8 minutes, open the lid and turn the ribs over. Close the lid and continue cooking.

14. Serve the beef and noodles, with the extra sauce on the side, if desired.

Carbonnade Flamande

Preparation time: 10 minutes

Cooking time: 1 hour

Overall time: 1 hour 10 minutes

Serves: 2 to 4 people

Recipe Ingredients:

- 2 lb. of brisket; cut into 2 or 3 pieces

- ¼ cup of beef broth
- 1 large onion; sliced
- 8 fluid ounces stout
- 1 teaspoon of olive oil
- 2 tablespoons of chopped fresh chervil
- ½ teaspoon of salt
- ½ teaspoon of Dijon-style mustard
- ½ teaspoon of brown sugar to taste
- ¼ teaspoon of dried rosemary leaves

Cooking Instructions:

1. Season the brisket with salt on all sides. On the Faboodi, select the Sear/Sauté function and adjust to Medium to preheat the innera pot.

2. Press the Start button and allow the pot to preheat for about 5 minutes. Heat the olive oil in the pot until shimmering and sear the brisket.

3. Cook, without turning, for about 4 minutes or until browned. Use tongs to turn the beef and move to the side.

4. Add the onion on the other side. Cook, stirring, for about 2 minutes or until slightly softened.

5. Pour in the stout, scraping off any browned bits from the bottom of the pot. Simmer and cook until the stout has reduced by about half.

6. Stir in the rosemary and broth. Seal the pressure lid, choose pressure; adjust the pressure to High and the cook time to 35 minutes.

7. Press the Start button. After cooking, perform a natural pressure release for about 10 minutes, then a quick release and carefully open the pressure lid.

8. Remove the beef onto a cutting board. Scoop off any excess fat on the sauce and stir in the mustard and brown sugar.

9. Select the Sear/Sauté button and adjust to Medium. Press Start. Simmer the sauce and cook until reduced to a thin gravy.

10. Taste and adjust the seasoning. Slice the beef and return to the sauce to reheat. Serve over mashed potatoes or noodles and garnish with chervil.

RICE, GRAINS AND PASTA RECIPES

Cherry Tomato Basil Linguine

Preparation time: 7 minutes

Cooking time: 15 minutes

Overall time: 22 minutes

Serves: 2 to 4 people

Recipe Ingredients:

- 1 lb. of Linguine noodles, halved
- 1 ½ cups of vegetable stock
- ¼ cup of julienned basil leaves
- ½ cup of Parmigiano-Reggiano cheese, grated
- 1 cup of cherry tomatoes, halved
- 1 small onion; diced
- 2 garlic cloves; minced
- 2 tablespoon of olive oil
- ¼ teaspoon of red chili flakes
- 1 teaspoon of salt
- ½ teaspoon of ground black pepper
- Fresh basil leaves for garnish

Cooking Instructions:

1. Warm oil on the Sear/Sauté function. Add onion and cook for about 2 minutes until soft. Mix garlic and tomatoes and sauté for about 4 minutes.

2. To the pot, add vegetable stock, salt, julienned basil, red chili flakes and pepper. Add linguine to the tomato mixture until covered.

3. Seal the pressure lid, choose Pressure, set to High, and set the timer to 5 minutes. Press the Start button.

4. When ready, naturally release the pressure for about 5 minutes. Stir the mixture to ensure it is broken down. Divide into plates.

5. Top with basil and Parmigiano-Reggiano cheese and serve.

Rigatoni with Spinach and Sausage

Preparation time: 15 minutes

Cooking time: 30 minutes

Overall time: 45 minutes

Serves: 2 to 4 people

Recipe Ingredients:

- 12 oz. of rigatoni pasta

- 4 sausage links; sliced
- 1 onion; chopped
- 3 cups of vegetable broth
- ¼ cup of tomato purée
- ½ cup of diced red bell pepper
- 1 cup of baby spinach
- ½ cup of Parmesan cheese
- 1 tablespoon of butter
- 2 teaspoons of chili powder
- Salt and ground black pepper to taste

Cooking Instructions:

1. Warm the butter on the Sear/Sauté function. Add red bell pepper, onion, and sausage, and cook for about 5 minutes.

2. Mix in vegetable broth, chili powder, tomato paste, salt, and pepper to combine. Stir in rigatoni pasta.

3. Seal the pressure lid, choose Pressure, set to High, and set the timer to 12 minutes. Press the Start button.

4. When ready, naturally release pressure for about 20 minutes. Stir in spinach and let simmer until wilted. Top with Parmesan cheese and serve.

Creamed Kale Parmesan Farro

Preparation time: 10 minutes

Cooking time: 25 minutes

Overall time: 35 minutes

Serves: 1 to 3 people

Recipe Ingredients:

- 1 cup of kale; chopped

- 2 cups of vegetable broth
- ½ cup of grated Parmesan cheese, plus 1 tbsp for topping
- 1 cup of pearl barley, rinsed and drained
- 1 small onion; diced
- 2 garlic cloves, smashed
- 1 tablespoon of butter
- Juice of ½ lemon, juiced
- Salt and freshly ground black pepper to taste

Cooking Instructions:

1. Warm butter on the Sear/Sauté function. Add in onion and cook for 3 minutes until soft.

2. Stir in garlic and barley, and cook for about 2 minutes until barley is toasted; mix in broth.

3. Seal the pressure lid, choose Pressure, set to High, and set the timer to 9 minutes. Press the Start button.

4. Release pressure naturally for about 10 minutes, then quick-release the remaining pressure. Add Parmesan cheese into barley mixture and stir until fully melted.

5. Just before serving, add lemon juice and kale into barley mixture. Add pepper and salt for seasoning.

Spicy Lentils with Chorizo.

Preparation time: 10 minutes

Cooking time: 40 minutes

Overall time: 50 minutes

Serves: 2 to 4 people

Recipe Ingredients:

- 7 oz. of chorizo; sliced

- 1 onion; diced
- 2 garlic cloves, crushed
- ½ cup of cider vinegar
- 2 cups of brown sugar
- 2 cups of lentils, drained and rinsed
- 2 cups of tomato sauce
- 2 cups of vegetable broth
- ½ cup of mustard
- 2 tablespoons of maple syrup
- 3 tablespoons of Worcestershire sauce
- 2 tablespoons of liquid smoke
- 1 tablespoon of lime juice
- 1 tablespoon of salt
- 1 tablespoon of black pepper
- 1 teaspoon of chili powder
- 1 teaspoon of paprika
- ¼ teaspoon of cayenne pepper

Cooking Instructions:

1. Switch on your Foodi to the Sear/Sauté function, set to Medium High, and press the Start/Stop button to preheat the po.

2. Add in chorizo and cook for about 3 minutes as you stir until crisp; add garlic and onion and cook for 2 more minutes until translucent.

3. Mix tomato sauce, broth, cider vinegar, liquid smoke, Worcestershire sauce, lime juice, mustard, and maple syrup in a mixing bowl.

4. Pour the mixture in the Foodi to deglaze the pan, scrape the bottom of the pan to do away with any browned bits of food.

5. Add pepper, chili powder, brown sugar, paprika, salt, and cayenne into the sauce mixture as you stir to mix.

6. Stir in lentils to coat, seal the pressure lid, choose Pressure, set to High, and set the timer to 30 minutes.

7. Press the Start button. When the time is up, release pressure naturally for about 10 minutes.

8. Serve immediately and enjoy!

Cheese and Spinach Stuffed Shells

Preparation time: 10 minutes

Cooking time: 50 minutes

Overall time: 1 hour

Serves: 2 to 4 people

Recipe Ingredients:

- 2 cups of onion; chopped
- 1 cup of shredded cheddar cheese

- 1 cup of carrot; chopped
- 2 cups of ricotta cheese, crumbled
- 1 ½ cup of feta cheese, crumbled
- 2 cups of spinach; chopped
- ¾ cup of grated Pecorino Romano cheese
- 1 (28 oz.) canned tomatoes, crushed
- 12 oz. of jumbo shell pasta
- 3 garlic cloves; minced
- 2 tablespoons of chopped fresh chives
- 1 tablespoon of chopped fresh dill
- 3 ½ tablespoons of olive oil
- 1 tablespoon of olive oil
- Salt and ground black pepper to taste

Cooking Instructions:

1. Warm olive oil on the Sear/Sauté function. Add in onion, carrot, and garlic, and cook for about 5 minutes until tender.

2. Stir in tomatoes and cook for another 10 minutes. Remove to a bowl and set it aside. Wipe the pot with a damp cloth, add pasta and cover with enough water.

3. Seal the pressure lid, choose Pressure, set to High, and set the timer to 5 minutes. Press the Start button.

4. Do a quick pressure and drain the pasta. Lightly grease olive oil to a baking sheet. In a bowl, combine feta and ricotta cheese.

5. Add in spinach, Pecorino Romano cheese, dill, and chives, and stir well. Adjust the seasonings.

6. Using a spoon, fill the shells with the mixture. Spread 4 cups tomato sauce on the baking sheet.

7. Place the stuffed shells over with seam-sides down and sprinkle cheddar cheese atop. Use aluminum foil to the cover the baking dish.

8. Pour 1 cup of water in the pot of the Foodi and insert the trivet. Lower the baking dish onto the trivet.

9. Seal the pressure lid, choose Pressure, set to High, and set the timer to 15 minutes. Press the Start button.

10. Once ready, do a quick release. Take away the foil. Place the stuffed shells to serving plates and top with tomato sauce before serving.

Beef Stuffed Pasta Shells

Preparation time: 10 minutes

Cooking time: 25 minutes

Overall time: 35 minutes

Serves: 2 to 4 people

Recipe Ingredients:

- 1 lb. of pound ground beef
- 16 oz. of pasta shells

- 10 oz. of red enchilada sauce
- 4 oz. of diced green chiles
- 15 oz. of tomato sauce
- 1 (15 oz.) can black beans, drained and rinsed
- 1(15 oz.) canned corn, drained
- 1 cup of shredded mozzarella cheese
- 2 cups of water
- 2 tablespoons of olive oil
- Finely chopped parsley for garnish
- Additional cheese for topping if desired
- Salt and ground black pepper to taste

Cooking Instructions:

1. Heat oil on the Sear/Sauté function, add ground beef and cook for about 7 minutes until it starts to brown.

2. Mix in pasta, tomato sauce, enchilada sauce, black beans, water, corn, and green chiles and stir to coat well.

3. Add more water if desired. Seal the pressure lid, choose Pressure, set to High, and set the timer to 10 minutes. Press the Start button.

4. When the time is up, do a quick pressure release. Into the pasta mixture, mix in mozzarella cheese until melted; add black pepper and salt.

5. Garnish with parsley to serve.

Black Eyed Peas with Kale

Preparation time: 10 minutes

Cooking time: 20 minutes

Overall time: 30 minutes

Serves: 2 to 4 people

Recipe Ingredients:

- 1 (15 oz.) can of fire roasted tomatoes
- 1 cup of fire-roasted red peppers; diced

- 1 ½ cups of dried black-eyed peas; soaked and rinsed
- 1 ½ cups of vegetable broth
- 2 cups of chopped kale
- 2 garlic cloves; minced
- 1 bay leaf
- 1 onion, thinly sliced
- ½ teaspoon of ground allspice
- 1 teaspoon of olive oil
- ½ teaspoon of red pepper, crushed
- Salt to taste

Cooking Instructions:

1. Warm oil on the Sear/Sauté function. Add onion and cook for about 5 minutes until fragrant.

2. Add garlic and fire roasted red peppers and cook for 1 more minute until softened. Add a seasoning of salt, crushed red pepper, and allspice to the vegetable mixture.

3. Add vegetable broth, bay leaf, and black-eyed peas to the pot. Seal the pressure lid, choose Pressure, set to High, and set the timer to 5 minutes.

4. Press the Start button. When the time is up, do a quick pressure release. Remove the bay leaf and discard.

5. Mix the peas with kale and tomatoes. Seal the pressure lid again, choose Pressure, set to High, and set the timer to 1 minute.

6. Press the Start button. When ready, release the pressure quickly. Adjust the seasoning and serve.

Turkey Fajita Tortiglioni

Preparation time: 10 minutes

Cooking time: 25 minutes

Overall time: 35 minutes

Serves: 2 to 4 people

Recipe Ingredients:

- 1 ½ lb. of turkey breast; cut into strips
- 16 oz. of tortiglioni

- 1 red bell pepper; sliced diagonally
- 1 yellow bell pepper; sliced diagonally
- 1 green bell pepper; sliced diagonally
- 1 medium red onion; cut into wedges
- 4 garlic cloves; minced
- 3 cups of chicken broth
- ½ cup of sour cream
- ½ cup of chopped parsley
- 1 cup of salsa
- 1 cup of shredded Gouda cheese
- 1 tablespoon of olive oil
- 2 teaspoons of chili powder
- 1 teaspoon of salt
- 1 teaspoon of cumin
- 1 teaspoon of onion powder
- 1 teaspoon of garlic powder
- ½ teaspoon of thyme

Cooking Instructions:

1. In a bowl, mix chili powder, cumin, garlic powder, onion powder, salt, and oregano.

2. Reserve 1 teaspoon of seasoning. Coat turkey with the remaining seasoning. Warm the oil on Sear/Sauté.

3. Add in turkey strips and cook for about 5 minutes until browned. Place the turkey in a bowl.

4. Cook the onion and garlic lightly for 1 minute until soft. In the Foodi, mix salsa and chicken broth, scrape the bottom of any brown bits.

5. Into the broth mixture, stir in tortiglioni pasta and cover with bell peppers and turkey.

6. Seal the pressure lid, choose Pressure, set to High, and set the timer to 5 minutes. Press the Start button.

7. When ready, do a quick pressure release. Open the lid and sprinkle with shredded gouda cheese and reserved seasoning and stir well.

8. Add more salt if desired. Divide into plates and top with sour cream. Add parsley for garnishing and serve.

Asian Yellow Lentils

Preparation time: 10 minutes

Cooking time: 20 minutes

Overall time: 30 minutes

Serves: 2 to 4 people

Recipe Ingredients:

- 1 tablespoon of ghee
- 2 teaspoon of cumin seeds
- 1 onion; chopped

- 4 garlic cloves; minced
- 1-inch piece of ginger, peeled; minced
- Sea salt salt
- 1 tomato; chopped
- 2 cups of split yellow lentils; soaked and drained
- 2 tablespoons of garam masala
- ½ teaspoon of ground turmeric
- ½ teaspoon of cayenne pepper
- 6 cups of water
- 1 tablespoon of fresh cilantro, finely chopped

Cooking Instructions:

1. Warm ghee on the Sear/Sauté function, set to Medium High, and press the Start/Stop button to preheat the pot.

2. Press the Start button and add cumin seeds and cook for about 10 seconds until they begin to pop, stir in onion and cook for 3 minutes until softened.

3. Mix in ginger and garlic and cook for 1 minute as you stir. Add salt for seasoning. Mix in tomato and cook for about 5 minutes until the mixture breaks down.

4. Stir in turmeric, lentils, garam masala, and cayenne and cover with water. Seal the pressure lid, choose Pressure, set to High, and set the timer to 8 minutes.

5. Press Start. When ready, release pressure quickly. Serve in bowls sprinkled with fresh cilantro.

Mix Bean Veggie Chili

Preparation time: 10 minutes

Cooking time: 50 minutes

Overall time: 1 hour

Serves: 2 to 4 people

Recipe Ingredients:

- ½ cup of dried pinto beans; soaked, drained and rinsed /65g
- ½ cup of dried black beans; soaked, drained and rinsed /65g

- ½ cup of dried cannellini beans; soaked, drained and rinsed /65g
- 4 cups of vegetable broth /1000ml
- 1 (28 oz.) can of tomatoes, crushed /840g
- 1 head of broccoli; chopped into florets
- 1 bay leaf
- 1 onion; chopped
- 3 stalks of celery; chopped
- 1 green bell pepper; chopped
- 1 tablespoon of canola oil /15ml
- 2 tablespoons of minced garlic /30g
- 2 tablespoons of chili powder /30g
- 2 teaspoons of ground cumin /10g
- Salt to taste
- Fresh parsley; chopped for garnish

Cooking Instructions:

1. Warm oil on the Sear/Sauté function. Add onion and bell pepper, broccoli, and celery, and cook for about 8 minutes until softened.

2. Mix in cumin, chili powder, and garlic and cook for another 1 minute. Add vegetable broth, tomatoes, black beans, salt, cannellini beans, pinto beans, and bay leaf to the pot.

3. Seal the pressure lid, choose Pressure, set to High, and set the timer to 25 minutes. Press the Start button.

4. When ready, do a quick pressure release. Dispose of the bay leaf. Taste and adjust the seasonings. Sprinkle with fresh parsley and serve.

Lemony Wild Rice Pilaf

Preparation time: 5 minutes

Cooking time: 20 minutes

Overall time: 25 minutes

Serves: 2 to 4 people

Recipe Ingredients:

- 2 cups of white wild rice, rinsed and drained
- 4 cups of vegetable broth /1000ml Zest and juice from 1 lemon

- 1 tablespoon of butter
- ½ teaspoon of salt
- ½ teaspoon of ground black pepper

Cooking Instructions:

1. In your Foodi, mix rice, lemon zest, butter, and water.

2. Seal the pressure lid, select the Pressure function, set to High, and set the timer to 3 minutes. Press the Start button.

3. When ready, release pressure naturally for about 10 minutes. Sprinkle salt, lemon juice, and pepper over the pilaf and use a fork to gently fluff.

Chicken Ragù Bolognese

Preparation time: 10 minutes

Cooking time: 40 minutes

Overall time: 50 minutes

Serves: 2 to 4 people

Recipe Ingredients:

- 1 ½ lb. of ground chicken

- 1 lb. of spaghetti
- 6 oz. of bacon; cubed
- ½ cup of white wine
- 1 cup of milk
- ¼ cup of tomato paste
- 1 cup of chicken broth
- 1 onion; minced
- 1 carrot; minced
- 1 celery stalk; minced
- 2 garlic cloves, crushed
- 2 tablespoons of olive oil
- ¼ teaspoon of crushed red pepper flakes
- Salt to taste

Cooking Instructions:

1. Warm oil on the Sear/Sauté function. Add in bacon and fry for about 5 minutes until crispy.

2. Add celery, carrot, garlic and onion and cook for about 5 minutes until fragrant. Mix in red pepper flakes and tomato paste and cook for about 2 minutes.

3. Break chicken into small pieces and place in the pot. Cook for about 10 minutes as you stir until browned. Pour in wine and simmer for about 2 minutes.

4. Add in chicken broth and milk. Seal the pressure lid, choose Pressure, set to High, and set the timer to 15 minutes.

5. Press Start. When ready, release the pressure quickly. Add in the spaghetti and stir.

6. Seal the pressure lid again, choose Pressure, set to High, and set the timer to another 5 minutes.

7. Press the Start button. When ready, release the pressure quickly. Check the pasta for doneness.

8. Press Sear/Sauté and cook for an additional 2 minutes if necessary. Adjust the seasoning and serve right away.

Lentil and Spinach

Preparation time: 5 minutes

Cooking time: 30 minutes

Overall time: 35 minutes

Serves: 2 to 4 people

Recipe Ingredients:

- 1 red jalapeño, seeded and minced
- 4 cloves of garlic; minced

- 1 tomato; diced
- 1½ cups of red lentils /195g
- ¼ cup of lemon juice /62.5ml
- 1 cup of spinach; chopped /130g
- 3 cups of water /750ml
- 1 tablespoon of cumin seeds /15g
- 2 tablespoons of olive oil /30ml
- 1 tablespoon of coriander seeds /15g
- 1 teaspoon of ground turmeric /5g
- ¼ teaspoon of cayenne pepper /1.25g
- 1 teaspoon of fresh ginger, peeled and grated /5g
- Fresh Cilantro; chopped for garnish
- Natural yogurt for garnish
- Salt to taste

Cooking Instructions:

1. Heat oil on the Sear/Sauté function, add cayenne pepper, jalapeño pepper, ginger, turmeric, cumin, and garlic, and coriander.

2. Cook for about 3 minutes until seeds become fragrant and begin to pop. Pour in water, tomato, and lentils into pot and stir.

3. Seal the pressure lid, choose Pressure, set to High, and set the timer to 10 minutes; press the Start.

4. Release pressure naturally for about 10 minutes, then turn steam vent valve to Venting to release the remaining pressure quickly.

5. Stir in spinach until wilted. Add lemon juice and season to taste. Divide lentils between bowls and garnish with yogurt and cilantro.

Pasta Caprese Ricotta Basil Fusilli

Preparation time: 5 minutes

Cooking time: 10 minutes

Overall time: 15 minutes

Serves: 1 to 3 people

Recipe Ingredients:

- 2 ½ cups of dried fusilli

- 1 (15 oz.) can of tomato sauce
- 1 cup of tomatoes, halved
- 1 cup of water
- ¼ cup of basil leaves
- 1 cup of Ricotta cheese, crumbled
- 1 onion, thinly sliced
- 6 garlic cloves; minced
- 1 tablespoon of olive oil
- 2 tablespoons of chopped fresh basil
- 1 teaspoon of red pepper flakes
- 1 teaspoon of salt

Cooking Instructions:

1. Warm the oil on the Sear/Sauté button. Add in red pepper flakes, garlic and onion and cook for about 3 minutes until soft.

2. Mix in fusilli, tomatoes, half of the basil leaves, water, tomato sauce, and salt. Seal the pressure lid, choose Pressure, set to High, and set the timer to 4 minutes.

3. Press the Start button. When ready, release the pressure quickly. Transfer the pasta to a serving platter.

4. Top with the crumbled ricotta and remaining chopped basil.

Grana Padano Risotto

Preparation time: 5 minutes

Cooking time: 20 minutes

Overall time: 25 minutes

Serves: 2 to 4 people

Recipe Ingredients:

- 1 white onion; chopped

- 2 cups of the Carnaroli rice, rinsed
- ¼ cup of dry white wine
- 4 cups of chicken stock
- 2 tablespoons of Grana Padano cheese, grated
- ¼ tablespoon of Grana Padano cheese, flakes
- 1 tablespoon of butter
- 1 tablespoon of olive oil
- 1 teaspoon of salt
- ½ teaspoon of ground white pepper

Cooking Instructions:

1. Warm oil on the Sear/Sauté function. Stir-fry onion for about 3 minutes until soft and translucent.

2. Add in butter and rice and cook for about 5 minutes stirring occasionally. Pour wine into the pot to deglaze.

3. Scrape away any browned bits of food from the pan. Stir in stock, pepper, and salt to the pot.

4. Seal the pressure lid, choose Pressure, set to High, and set the timer to 15 minutes. Press the Start button.

5. When ready, release the pressure quickly. Sprinkle with grated Parmesan cheese and stir well.

6. Top with flaked cheese for garnish before serving.

SNACKS, APPETIZERS AND SIDES

Chicken and Cheese Bake

Preparation time: 18 minutes

Cooking time: 1 hour

Overall time: 1 hour 18 minutes

Serves: 2 to 4 people

Recipe Ingredients:

- 1 pound of chicken breast /450g
- 10 ounces of Cheddar cheese /300g
- 10 ounces of cream cheese /300g
- ½ cup of sour cream /125ml
- ½ cup of breadcrumbs /65g
- ½ cup of water /125ml

Cooking Instructions:

1. Open the Ninja Foodi and add the chicken, water, and cream cheese.

2. Close the lid, secure the pressure valve, and select Pressure mode on High for about 10 minutes.

3. Press the Start/Stop button. Once the timer has ended, do a quick pressure release, and open the pot.

4. Shred the chicken with two forks and add the cheddar cheese. Sprinkle with breadcrumbs, and close the crisping lid.

5. Select the Bake/Roast function, set the temperature to 380°F and the timer to 3 minutes. Serve warm with veggie bites.

Mouthwatering Meatballs

Preparation time: 10 minutes

Cooking time: 20 minutes

Overall time: 30 minutes

Serves: 2 to 4 people

Recipe Ingredients:

- 2 pound of ground beef

- 1 potato, shredded
- 2 eggs, beaten
- ½ cup of Parmesan cheese, grated
- 2 cups of tomato sauce to serve
- 2 tablespoons of chopped chives
- ¼ teaspoon of pepper
- ½ teaspoon of garlic powder
- ½ teaspoon of salt
- 1 package of cooked spaghetti to serve
- Basil leaves to serve
- Cooking spray

Cooking Instructions:

1. In a large bowl, combine the potato, salt, pepper, garlic powder, eggs, and chives.

2. Form 12 balls out of the mixture. Spray with cooking spray. Arrange half of the balls onto a lined Ninja Foodi basket.

3. Close the crisping lid and cook for about 14 minutes on the Air Crisp function at 330°F. After 7 minutes, turn the meatballs.

4. Repeat with the other half. Serve over cooked spaghetti mixed with tomato sauce, sprinkled with Parmesan cheese and basil leaves.

Fried Beef Dumplings

Preparation time: 15 minutes

Cooking time: 30 minutes

Overall time: 45 minutes

Serves: 2 to 4 people

Recipe Ingredients:

- 8 oz. of ground beef

- 20 wonton wrappers
- 1 carrot, grated
- 1 large egg, beaten
- 1 garlic clove, minced
- ½ cup of grated cabbage
- 2 tablespoons of olive oil
- 2 tablespoons of coconut aminos
- ½ tablespoon of melted ghee
- ½ tablespoon of ginger powder
- ½ teaspoon of salt
- ½ teaspoon of freshly ground black pepper

Cooking Instructions:

1. Put the Crisping Basket in the pot. Close the crisping lid, select the Air Crisp function, set the temperature to 400°F, and the time to 5 minutes.

2. Press the Start/Stop button. In a large bowl, mix the beef, cabbage, carrot, egg, garlic, coconut aminos, ghee, ginger, salt, and black pepper.

3. Put the wonton wrappers on a clean flat surface and spoon 1 tablespoon of the beef mixture into the middle of each wrapper.

4. Run the edges of the wrapper with a little water; fold the wrapper to cover the filling into a semi-circle shape and pinch the edges to seal.

5. Brush the dumplings with olive oil. Lay the dumplings in the preheated basket, select the Air Crisp function, set the temperature to 400°F.

6. Set the time to 12 minutes. Press the Start/Stop button to begin frying. After 6 minutes, open the lid, pull out the basket and shake the dumplings.

7. Return the basket to the pot and close the lid to continue frying until the dumplings are crispy to your desire.

Rosemary and Garlic Mushrooms

Preparation time: 10 minutes

Cooking time: 10 minutes

Overall time: 20 minutes

Serves: 2 to 4 people

Recipe Ingredients:

- 12 ounces of button mushrooms /360g
- 2 rosemary sprigs
- 3 garlic cloves, minced
- ¼ cup of melted butter /62.5ml
- ½ teaspoon of salt /2.5g
- ¼ teaspoon of black pepper /1.25g

Cooking Instructions:

1. Wash and pat dry the mushrooms and cut them in half. Place in a large bowl.

2. Add the remaining Ingredients to the bowl and toss well to combine. Transfer the mushrooms to the basket of the Ninja Foodi.

3. Close the crisping lid and cook for about 12 minutes on the Air Crisp function, shaking once halfway through; at 350°F.

Cumin Baby Carrots

Preparation time: 5 minutes

Cooking time: 20 minutes

Overall time: 25 minutes

Serves: 2 to 4 people

Recipe Ingredients:

- 1 ¼ pounds of baby carrots
- 1 handful cilantro; chopped
- 2 tablespoons of olive oil
- ½ teaspoon of cumin powder
- ½ teaspoon of garlic powder
- 1 teaspoon of cumin seeds
- 1 teaspoon of salt
- ½ teaspoon of black pepper

Cooking Instructions:

1. Place the baby carrots in a large bowl. Add cumin seeds, cumin, olive oil, salt, garlic powder, and pepper, and stir to coat them well.

2. Put the carrots in the Ninja Foodi's basket, close the crisping lid and cook for about 20 minutes on the Roast function at 370°F.

3. Remove to a platter and sprinkle with chopped cilantro, to serve.

Green Vegan Dip

Preparation time: 5 minutes

Cooking time: 15 minutes

Overall time: 20 minutes

Serves: 2 to 4 people

Recipe Ingredients:

- 10 oz. of canned green chiles, drained with liquid reserved
- 2 cups of broccoli florets
- ¼ cup of raw cashews
- ¼ cup of soy sauce
- 1 cup of water
- ¾ cup of green bell pepper; chopped
- ¼ teaspoon of garlic powder
- ½ teaspoon of sea salt
- ¼ teaspoon of chili powder

Cooking Instructions:

1. In the cooker, add cashews, broccoli, green bell pepper, and water.

2. Seal the pressure lid, select the Pressure function, set to High, and set the timer to 5 minutes.

3. Press the Start button. When ready, release the pressure quickly. Drain water from the pot.

4. Add reserved liquid from canned green chilies, sea salt, garlic powder, chili powder, soy sauce, and cumin.

5. Use an immersion blender to blend the mixture until smooth; set aside in a mixing bowl.

6. Stir green chilies through the dip; add your desired optional additions.

Fried Pin Wheels

Preparation time: 10 minutes

Cooking time: 40 minutes

Overall time: 50 minutes

Serves: 2 to 4 people

Recipe Ingredients:

- 1 sheet puff pastry
- 1 ½ cups of Gruyere cheese, grated
- 8 ham slices
- 4 teaspoons of Dijon mustard

Cooking Instructions:

1. Place the pastry on a lightly floured flat surface. Brush the mustard over and arrange the ham slices; top with cheese.

2. Start at the shorter edge and roll up the pastry. Wrap it in a plastic foil and place in the freezer for about half an hour, until it becomes firm and comfortable to cut.

3. Meanwhile, slice the pastry into 6 rounds. Line the Ninja Foodi basket with parchment paper, and arrange the pinwheels on top.

4. Close the crisping lid and cook for 10 minutes on the Air Crisp function at 370°F. Leave to cool on a wire rack before serving.

Honey Mustard Hot Dogs

Preparation time: 5 minutes

Cooking time: 17 minutes

Overall time: 22 minutes

Serves: 2 to 4 people

Recipe Ingredients:

- 20 Hot Dogs, cut into 4 pieces
- ¼ cup of honey /62.5ml
- ¼ cup of red wine vinegar /62.5ml
- ½ cup of tomato puree /125ml
- ¼ cup of water /62.5ml
- 1½ teaspoon of soy sauce /7.5ml
- 1 teaspoon of Dijon mustard /5g
- Salt and black pepper to taste

Cooking Instructions:

1. Add the tomato puree, red wine vinegar, honey, soy sauce, Dijon mustard, salt, and black pepper in a medium bowl.

2. Mix them with a spoon. Put sausage weenies in the crisp basket, and close the crisping lid.

3. Select the Air Crisp function, set the temperature to 370 °F or 188°C and the timer to 4 minutes.

4. Press the Start/Stop button. At the 2-minute mark, turn the sausages. Once ready, open the lid and pour the sweet sauce over the sausage weenies.

5. Close the pressure lid, secure the pressure valve, and select Pressure mode on High for about 3 minutes.

6. Press the Start/Stop button. Once the timer has ended, do a quick pressure release. Serve immediately and enjoy.

Artichoke Bites

Preparation time: 10 minutes

Cooking time: 1 hour

Overall time: 1 hour 10 minutes

Serves: 2 to 4 people

Recipe Ingredients:

- ¼ cup of frozen chopped kale
- ¼ cup of finely chopped artichoke hearts
- ¼ cup of goat cheese
- ¼ cup of ricotta cheese
- 4 (13-by-18-inch) sheets frozen phyllo dough, thawed
- 1 lemon, zested
- 1 large egg white
- 1 tablespoon of olive oil
- 2 tablespoons of grated Parmesan cheese
- 1 teaspoon of dried basil
- ½ teaspoon of salt
- ½ teaspoon of freshly ground black pepper

Cooking Instructions:

1. In a bowl, mix the kale, artichoke hearts, ricotta cheese, parmesan cheese, goat cheese, egg white, basil, lemon zest, salt, and pepper.

2. Put the Crisping Basket in the pot. Close the crisping lid, choose Air Crisp, set the temperature to 375°F, and the time to 5 minutes; press the Start/Stop button.

3. Then, place a phyllo sheet on a clean flat surface. Brush with olive oil, place a second phyllo sheet on the first, and brush with oil.

4. Continue layering to form a pile of four oiled sheets. Working from the short side, cut the phyllo sheets into 8 strips.

5. Cut the strips in half to form 16 strips. Spoon 1 tablespoon of filling onto one short side of every strip.

6. Fold a corner to cover the filling to make a triangle; continue repeatedly folding to the end of the strip, creating a triangle-shaped phyllo packet.

7. Repeat the process with the other phyllo bites. Open the crisping lid and place half of the pastry in the basket in a single layer.

8. Close the lid, Choose Air Crisp, set the temperature to 350°F, and the timer to 12 minutes; press the Start/Stop button.

9. After 6 minutes, open the lid, and flip the bites. Return the basket to the pot and close the lid to continue baking.

10. When ready, take out the bites into a plate. Serve warm.

Creamy Tomato Parsley Dip

Preparation time: 5 minutes

Cooking time: 15 minutes

Overall time: 18 minutes

Serves: 2 to 4 people

Recipe Ingredients:

- 10 ounces of shredded Parmesan cheese
- 10 ounces cream cheese
- ½ cup of heavy cream
- 1 cup of chopped tomatoes
- 1 cup of water
- ¼ cup of chopped parsley

Cooking Instructions:

1. Open the Ninja Foodi and pour in the tomatoes, parsley, heavy cream, cream cheese, and water.

2. Close the lid, secure the pressure valve, and select Pressure for about 3 minutes at High. Press the Start/Stop function.

3. Once the timer has ended, do a natural pressure release for about 10 minutes. Stir the mixture with a spoon while mashing the tomatoes with the back of the spoon.

4. Add the parmesan cheese and close the crisping lid. Select the Bake/Roast function, set the temperature to 370°F°C and the time to 3 minutes.

5. Dish the dip into a bowl and serve with chips or veggie bites.

Crispy Cheesy Straws

Preparation time: 15 minutes

Cooking time: 30 minutes

Overall time: 45 minutes

Serves: 2 to 4 people

Recipe Ingredients:

- 2 cups of cauliflower florets, steamed
- 5 ounces of cheddar cheese
- 3 ½ ounces of oats
- 1 egg
- 1 red onion; diced
- 1 teaspoon of mustard
- Salt and pepper, to taste

Cooking Instructions:

1. Add the oats in a food processor and process until they resemble breadcrumbs.

2. Place the steamed florets in a cheesecloth and squeeze out the excess liquid. Put the florets in a large bowl, and add the rest of the ingredients to the bowl.

3. Mix well with your hands, to combine the ingredients thoroughly. Take a little bit of the mixture and twist it into a straw.

4. Place in the lined Ninja Foodi basket; repeat with the rest of the mixture. Close the crisping lid and cook for about 10 minutes on Air Crisp mode at 350°F.

5. After 5 minutes, turn them over and cook for an additional 10 minutes.

Barbecue Chicken Drumsticks

Preparation time: 10 minutes

Cooking time: 20 minutes

Overall time: 30 minutes

Serves: 2 to 4 people

Recipe Ingredients:

- 3 pound of chicken drumsticks
- 1 cup of Barbecue sauce
- ¼ cup of butter, melted
- ½ cup of water
- 3 tablespoons of garlic powder
- Salt to taste

Cooking Instructions:

1. Season drumsticks with garlic powder and salt. Open the Ninja Foodi, pour in the water, and fit in the reversible rack.

2. Arrange the drumsticks on top, close the lid, secure the pressure valve, and select Pressure mode for about 5 minutes.

3. Press the Start/Stop button to start cooking. Once the timer has ended, do a natural pressure release for about 10 minutes.

4. When the time is up, do a quick pressure release to let out any more steam. Open the lid.

5. Remove the drumsticks to a crisp basket and add the butter and half of the barbecue sauce.

6. Stir the chicken until well coated in the sauce. Insert the basket in the pot and close the crisping lid.

7. Select the Air Crisp function, set to 380 °F, and cook for 10 minutes. Press the Start/Stop button.

8. Once it is nice and crispy, remove drumsticks to a bowl, and top with the remaining barbecue sauces. Stir and serve the chicken with a cheese dip.

Cheesy Brazilian Balls

Preparation time: 10 minutes

Cooking time: 25 minutes

Overall time: 35 minutes

Serves: 2 to 4 people

Recipe Ingredients:

- 2 cups of flour
- 2 cups of grated mozzarella cheese /260g
- ½ cup of olive oil /125ml
- 1 cup of milk /250ml
- 2 eggs, cracked into a bowl
- A pinch of salt

Cooking Instructions:

1. Grease the crisp basket with cooking spray and set aside.

2. Put the Ninja Foodi on Medium and select the Sear/Sauté function. Add the milk, oil, and salt, and let boil. Add the flour and mix it vigorously with a spoon.

3. Let the mixture cool. Once cooled, use a hand mixer to mix the dough well, and add the eggs and cheese while still mixing.

4. The dough should be thick and sticky. Use your hands to make 14 balls out of the mixture, and put them in the greased basket.

5. Put the basket in the pot and close the crisping lid. Select Air Crisp, set the temperature to 380°F and set the timer to 15 minutes.

6. At the 7-minute mark, shake the balls. Serve with lemon aioli, garlic mayo or ketchup.

Cheesy Smashed Sweet Potatoes

Preparation time: 10 minutes

Cooking time: 1 hour

Overall time: 1 hour 10 minutes

Serves: 2 to 4 people

Recipe Ingredients:

- 2 slices of bacon, cooked and crumbled
- 12 oz. of baby sweet potatoes
- ¼ cup of shredded Monterey Jack cheese
- ¼ cup of sour cream
- 1 tablespoon of chopped scallions
- 1 teaspoon of melted butter
- Salt to taste

Cooking Instructions:

1. Put the Crisping Basket in the pot and close the crisping lid.

2. Select the Air Crisp function and set the temperature to 350°F, and the time to 5 minutes.

3. Press the Start/Stop button to begin preheating. Meanwhile, toss the sweet potatoes with the melted butter until evenly coated.

4. Once the pot and basket have preheated, open the lid and add the sweet potatoes to the basket.

5. Close the lid, select the Air Crisp function and set the temperature to 350°F, and set the time to 30 minutes; press the Start button.

6. After 15 minutes, open the lid, pull out the basket and shake the sweet potatoes. Return the basket to the pot and close the lid to continue cooking.

7. When ended, check the sweet potatoes for your desired crispiness, which should also be fork tender.

8. Take out the sweet potatoes from the basket and use a large spoon to crush the soft potatoes just to split lightly.

9. Top with the cheese, sour cream, bacon, and scallions, and season with salt.

Cheesy Tomato Bruschetta

Preparation time: 5 minutes

Cooking time: 10 minutes

Overall time: 15 minutes

Serves: 1 to 3 people

Recipe Ingredients:

- 1 Italian Ciabatta Sandwich Bread
- 2 tomatoes; chopped
- 2 garlic cloves, minced
- 1 cup of grated mozzarella cheese /130g
- Olive oil to brush
- Basil leaves; chopped
- Salt and pepper to taste

Cooking Instructions:

1. Cut the bread in half, lengthways, then each piece again in half.

2. Drizzle each bit with olive oil and sprinkle with garlic. Top with the grated cheese, salt, and pepper.

3. Place the bruschetta pieces into the Ninja Foodi basket, close the crisping lid and cook for about 12 minutes on the Air Crisp function at 380°F.

4. At 6 minutes, check for doneness. Once the Ninja Foodi beeps, remove the bruschetta to a serving platter.

5. Spoon over the tomatoes and chopped basil to serve.

VEGETABLES AND VEGAN RECIPES
Roasted Squash and Rice with Crispy Tofu

Preparation time: 10 minutes

Cooking time: 1 hour

Overall time: 1 hour 10 minutes

Serves: 2 to 4 people

Recipe Ingredients:

- 1 small butternut squash, peeled and diced
- 1 (15 oz.) block of extra-firm tofu, drained and cubed
- 1 cup of jasmine rice, cooked
- ¾ cup of water
- 1 tablespoon of coconut aminos
- 2 tablespoons of melted butter; divided
- 2 teaspoons of arrowroot starch
- 1 teaspoon of salt
- 1 teaspoon of freshly ground black pepper

Cooking Instructions:

1. Pour the rice and water into the pot and mix with a spoon. Seal the pressure lid, choose Pressure, set to High and set the time to 2 minutes.

2. Select the Start/Stop button to boil the rice. in a bowl, toss the butternut squash with 1 tbsp of melted butter and season with the salt and black pepper, set it aside.

3. In another bowl, mix the remaining butter with the coconut aminos, and toss the tofu in the mixture.

4. Pour the arrowroot starch over the tofu and toss again to combine well. When done cooking the rice, perform a quick pressure release.

5. Carefully open the pressure lid. Put the reversible rack in the pot in the higher position and line with aluminum foil.

6. Arrange the tofu and butternut squash on the rack. Close the crisping lid. Select the Air Crisp function at 400°F and set the time to 20 minutes.

7. Press the Start/Stop button to begin cooking. After 10 minutes, use tongs to turn the butternut squash and tofu.

8. When done cooking, check for your desired crispiness and serve the tofu and squash with the rice.

Quinoa Pesto Bowls with Veggies

Preparation time: 10 minutes

Cooking time: 20 minutes

Overall time: 30 minutes

Serves: 1 to 3 people

Recipe Ingredients:

- 1 cup of quinoa, rinsed
- 1 cup of broccoli florets
- ¼ cup of pesto sauce
- 2 cups of water
- ½ lb. of Brussels sprouts
- 2 eggs
- 1 small beet, peeled and cubed
- 1 carrot, peeled and chopped
- 1 avocado, thinly sliced
- lemon wedges; for serving
- Salt and ground black pepper to taste

Cooking Instructions:

1. In the pot, mix water, salt, quinoa and pepper. Set the reversible rack to the pot over quinoa.

2. Add eggs, Brussels sprouts, broccoli, beet cubes, carrots, pepper and salt to the reversible rack.

3. Seal the pressure lid, choose Pressure, set to High, and set the timer to 1 minute. Press the Start button.

4. Release pressure naturally for about 10 minutes, then release any remaining pressure quickly.

5. Remove reversible rack from the pot and set the eggs to a bowl of ice water. Peel and halve the eggs. Use a fork to fluff quinoa.

6. Separate quinoa, broccoli, avocado, carrots, beet, Brussels sprouts, eggs, and a dollop of pesto into two bowls. Serve alongside a lemon wedge.

Olives and Rice Stuffed Mushrooms

Preparation time: 10 minutes

Cooking time: 1 hour

Overall time: 1 hour 10 minutes

Serves: 2 to 4 people

Recipe Ingredients:

- 4 large Portobello mushrooms, stems and gills removed
- 1 green bell pepper, seeded and diced
- 1 lemon, juiced
- 1 tomato, seed removed and chopped
- ½ cup of brown rice, cooked
- ¼ cup of black olives, pitted and chopped
- ½ cup of feta cheese, crumbled
- 2 tablespoons of melted butter
- ½ teaspoon of salt
- ½ teaspoon of ground black pepper
- Minced fresh cilantro; for garnish

Cooking Instructions:

1. Put the Crisping Basket in the pot. Close the crisping lid, select the Air Crisp, setting the temperature to 375°F, and setting the time to 5 minutes.

2. Press the Start/Stop button to preheat the pot. Brush the mushrooms with the melted butter. Open the crisping lid and arrange the mushrooms, open-side up and in a single layer in the preheated basket.

3. Close the crisping lid. Select the Air Crisp function, set the temperature to 375°F, and set the time to 20 minutes. Press the Start/Stop button.

4. In a bowl, combine the brown rice, tomato, olives, bell pepper, feta cheese, lemon juice, salt, and black pepper. Open the crisping lid and spoon the rice mixture equally into the 4 mushrooms. Close the lid.

5. Choose Air Crisp, set the temperature to 350°F, and set the time to 8 minutes. Press the Start/Stop button to commence cooking.

6. When the mushrooms are ready, remove to a plate, garnish with fresh cilantro and serve immediately.

Zucchini Quinoa Stuffed Red Peppers

Preparation time: 10 minutes

Cooking time: 30 minutes

Overall time: 40 minutes

Serves: 2 to 4 people

Recipe Ingredients:

- 1 small zucchini; chopped
- 4 red bell peppers
- 2 large tomatoes; chopped
- 1 small onion; chopped
- 2 cloves of garlic, minced
- 1 cup of quinoa, rinsed /130g
- 1 cup of grated Gouda cheese /130g
- ½ cup of chopped mushrooms /65g
- 1 ½ cup of water /375ml
- 2 cups of chicken broth /500ml
- 1 tablespoon of olive oil /15ml
- ½ teaspoon of smoked paprika /2.5g
- Salt and black pepper to taste

Cooking Instructions:

1. Select the Sear/Sauté function on High mode. Once it is ready, add the olive oil to heat and then add the onion and garlic.

2. Sauté for about 3 minutes to soften, stirring occasionally. Include the tomatoes, cook for about 3 minutes and then add the quinoa, zucchinis, and mushrooms.

3. Season with paprika, salt, and black pepper and stir with a spoon. Cook for about 7 minutes, then, turn the pot off.

4. Use a knife to cut the bell peppers in halves (lengthwise) and remove their seeds and stems.

5. Spoon the quinoa mixture into the bell peppers. Put the peppers in a greased baking dish and pour the broth over.

6. Wipe the pot clean with some paper towels, and pour the water into it. After, fit the steamer rack at the bottom of the pot.

7. Place the baking dish on top of the reversible rack, cover with aluminum foil, close the lid, secure the pressure valve.

8. Select the Pressure function on High pressure for about 15 minutes. Press the Start/Stop button.

9. Once the timer has ended, do a quick pressure release and open the lid. Remove the aluminum foil and sprinkle with the gouda cheese.

10. Close the crisping lid, select the Bake/Roast function mode and cook for about 10 minutes on 375°F.

11. Arrange the stuffed peppers on a serving platter and serve right away or as a side to a meat dish.

Aloo Gobi with Cilantro

Preparation time: 10 minutes

Cooking time: 30 minutes

Overall time: 40 minutes

Serves: 2 to 4 people

Recipe Ingredients:

- 1 head of cauliflower, cored and cut into florets
- 1 potato, peeled and diced
- 4 garlic cloves, minced
- 1 tomato, cored and chopped
- 1 jalapeño pepper, deseeded and minced
- 1 onion, minced
- 1 cup of water
- 1 tablespoon of curry paste
- 1 tablespoon of vegetable oil
- 1 tablespoon of ghee
- 2 teaspoons of cumin seeds
- 1 teaspoon of ground turmeric
- ½ teaspoon of chili pepper
- Salt to taste
- A handful of cilantro leaves; chopped

Cooking Instructions:

1. Warm oil on the Sear/Sauté function and add in potato and cauliflower and cook for about 10 minutes until lightly browned; add salt for seasoning.

2. Set the vegetables to a bowl. Add ghee to the pot. Mix in cumin seeds and cook for about 10 seconds until they start to pop.

3. Add onion and cook for about 3 minutes until softened. Mix in garlic; cook for seconds.

4. Add in tomato, curry paste, chili pepper, jalapeño pepper, curry paste, and turmeric; cook for about 5 minutes until the tomato starts to break down.

5. Return potato and cauliflower to the pot. Add water over the vegetables, add more salt if needed, and stir.

6. Seal the pressure lid, choose Pressure, set to High, and set the timer to 4 minutes. Press the Start button.

7. Release pressure naturally. Top with cilantro and serve.

Pumpkin Soup

Preparation time: 10 minutes

Cooking time: 20 minutes

Overall time: 30 minutes

Serves: 2 to 4 people

Recipe Ingredients:

- 1 pound of green beans, cut in 5 strips each
- 16 ounces pumpkin puree
- 1 celeriac, peeled and cubed
- 5 stalks celery; chopped
- 1 white onion; chopped
- 2 cups of vegetable broth
- 3 cups of spinach leaves
- 1 tablespoon of chopped basil leaves
- ¼ teaspoon of dried thyme
- ⅛ teaspoon of rubbed sage
- Salt to taste

Cooking Instructions:

1. Open the Ninja Foodi and pour in the celeriac, pumpkin puree, celery, onion, green beans, vegetable broth, basil leaves, thyme, sage, and a little salt.

2. Close the lid, secure the pressure valve, and select Steam mode on High pressure for about 5 minutes.

3. Press the Start/Stop button. Once the timer has ended, do a quick pressure release and open the lid.

4. Add in the spinach and stir using a spoon. Close the crisping lid and cook for about 3 minutes on the Broil function.

5. Use a soup spoon to fetch the soup into serving bowls.

Mushroom Risotto with Swiss Chard

Preparation time: 10 minutes

Cooking time: 50 minutes

Overall time: 1 hour

Serves: 2 to 4 people

Recipe Ingredients:

- 1 small bunch Swiss chard; chopped
- ½ cup of sautéed mushrooms
- ½ cup of caramelized onions
- ⅓ cup of white wine
- 2 cups of vegetable stock
- ⅓ cup of grated Pecorino Romano cheese
- 1 cup of short grain rice
- 3 tablespoons of ghee; divided
- ½ teaspoon of salt

Cooking Instructions:

1. Select the Sear/Sauté function and adjust to Medium. Press Start to preheat the inner pot.

2. Melt 2 tablespoons of ghee and sauté the Swiss chard for about 5 minutes until wilted.

3. Spoon into a bowl and set aside. Use a paper towel to wipe out any remaining liquid in the pot and melt the remaining ghee. Stir in the rice and cook for about 1 minute.

4. Add the white wine and cook for about 3 minutes, with occasional stirring until the wine has evaporated.

5. Add in stock and salt; stir to combine. Seal the pressure lid, choose Pressure; adjust the pressure to High and the cook time to 8 minutes; press the Start button.

6. When the timer is done reading, perform a quick pressure release and carefully open the lid.

7. Stir in the mushrooms, swiss chard, and onions and let the risotto heat for about 2 minutes.

8. Mix the cheese into the rice to melt, and adjust the taste with salt. Spoon the risotto into serving bowls and serve immediately.

Rice Stuffed Zucchini Boats

Preparation time: 10 minutes

Cooking time: 45 minutes

Overall time: 55 minutes

Serves: 2 to 4 people

Recipe Ingredients:

- 2 small zucchinis
- ½ cup of chopped toasted cashew nuts
- ½ cup of grated Parmesan cheese; divided
- ½ cup of cooked white short grain rice
- ½ cup of canned white beans, drained and rinsed
- ½ cup of chopped tomatoes
- 2 tablespoons of melted butter; divided
- ½ teaspoon of salt
- ½ teaspoon of freshly ground black pepper

Cooking Instructions:

1. Cut each zucchini in half and then, cut in half lengthwise and scoop out the pulp. Chop the pulp roughly and place in a medium bowl.

2. In the bowl, add the rice, beans, tomatoes, cashew nuts, ¼ cup of Parmesan cheese, 1 tbsp or 15mlof melted butter, the salt, and black pepper.

3. Combine the mixture well but not to break the beans. Put the Crisping Basket in the pot.

4. Close the crisping lid, select the Air Crisp function, set the temperature to 400°F, and the time to 5 minutes.

5. Spoon the mixed Ingredients into the zucchini boats and arrange the stuffed zucchinis in a single layer in the preheated basket.

6. Close the crisping lid. Select Air Crisp function, set the temperature to 400°F, and the time to 15 minutes.

7. Press the Start/Stop to begin cooking. After 15 minutes, sprinkle the zucchini boats with the remaining Parmesan cheese and butter.

8. Close the crisping lid. Choose Broil, set the time to 5 minutes, and press Start/Stop button to broil.

9. When done cooking, ensure it is as crisp as you desire, otherwise broil for a few more minutes.

10. Remove the zucchinis onto a plate, allow cooling for about a minute, and serve.

Prawn Toast

Preparation time: 5 minutes

Cooking time: 10 minutes

Overall time: 15 minutes

Serves: 1 to 3 people

Recipe Ingredients:

- 6 large prawns, shells removed; chopped
- 1 egg white, whisked
- 1 large spring onion, finely sliced
- ½ cup of sweet corn /65g
- 3 white slices of bread
- 1 tablespoon of black sesame seeds /15g

Cooking Instructions:

1. In a bowl, place the prawns, corn, spring onion and the black sesame seeds. Add the whisked egg white, and mix the ingredients.

2. Spread the mixture over the bread slices. Place the prawns in the Ninja Foodi's basket and sprinkle with oil.

3. Close the crisping lid and fry the prawns until golden; for about 10 minutes at 370°F on the Air Crisp function.

4. Serve with ketchup or chili sauce.

Eggplant Lasagna

Preparation time: 5 minutes

Cooking time: 20 minutes

Overall time: 25 minutes

Serves: 2 to 4 people

Recipe Ingredients:

- 3 large eggplants; sliced in uniform ¼ inches
- ¼ cup of Parmesan cheese, grated
- 4 ¼ cups of Marinara sauce
- 1 ½ cups of shredded Mozzarella cheese
- Cooking spray
- Chopped fresh basil to garnish

Cooking Instructions:

1. Open the pot and grease it with cooking spray. Arrange the eggplant slices in a single layer on the bottom of the pot and sprinkle some cheese all over it.

2. Arrange another layer of eggplant slices on the cheese, sprinkle this layer with cheese also.

3. Repeat the layering of eggplant and cheese until both Ingredients are exhausted. Lightly spray the eggplant with cooking spray, pour the marinara sauce all over it.

4. Close the lid and pressure valve, and select the Pressure function on High pressure for about 8 minutes.

5. Press the Start/Stop button. Once the timer has stopped, do a quick pressure release, and open the lid.

6. Sprinkle with grated parmesan cheese, close the crisping lid and cook for about 10 minutes on the Bake/Roast function at 380°F.

7. With two napkins in hand, gently remove the inner pot. Allow cooling for about 10 minutes before serving.

8. Garnish the lasagna with basil and serve warm as a side dish.

Crispy Kale Chips

Preparation time: 5 minutes

Cooking time: 5 minutes

Overall time: 10 minutes

Serves: 1 to 3 people

Recipe Ingredients:

- 4 cups of kale, stemmed and packed /520g
- 1 tablespoon of yeast flakes /15g
- 2 tablespoons of olive oil /30ml
- 1 teaspoon of vegan seasoning /5g
- Salt to taste

Cooking Instructions:

1. In a bowl, add the oil, the kale, the vegan seasoning, and the yeast and mix well. Dump the coated kale in the Ninja Foodi's basket.

2. Set the heat to 370°F, close the crisping lid and fry for a total of 6 minutes on Air Crisp mode.

3. Shake it from time to time. Serve immediately and enjoy!

Carrots with Crumbled Bacon

Preparation time: 10 minutes

Cooking time: 20 minutes

Overall time: 30 minutes

Serves: 2 to 4 people

Recipe Ingredients:

- 4 lb. of carrots, peeled and sliced
- ½ cup of fresh orange juice
- ¼ cup of olive oil
- 3 slices of bacon, crumbled
- 1 tablespoon of cold water
- 3 tablespoons of honey
- 1 teaspoon of salt
- 2 teaspoons of cornstarch

Cooking Instructions:

1. Fry the bacon in your pressure cooker on Sear/Sauté until crisp, for about 5 minutes and set it aside.

2. In a bowl, mix salt, olive oil, orange juice, and maple syrup; add the mixture and carrots to the pot and mix well to coat.

3. Seal the pressure lid, choose Pressure, set to High, and set the timer to 6 minutes. Press the Start button.

4. When ready, release the pressure quickly. Transfer carrots to a serving dish. Select the Sear/Sauté function.

5. In a bowl, mix cold water and cornstarch until cornstarch dissolves completely; add to the liquid remaining in the pressure cooker.

6. Simmer sauce as you stir for about 2 minutes to obtain a thick and smooth consistency.

7. Ladle sauce over the carrots and scatter over the crumbled bacon.

Mashed Broccoli with Cream Cheese

Preparation time: 5 minutes

Cooking time: 10 minutes

Overall time: 15 minutes

Serves: 2 to 4 people

Recipe Ingredients:

- 3 heads of broccoli; chopped
- 2 cloves of garlic, crushed
- 6 ounces of cream cheese
- 2 cups of water
- 2 tablespoons of butter, unsalted
- Salt and black pepper to taste

Cooking Instructions:

1. Turn on the Ninja Foodi and select the Sear/Sauté function, adjust to High.

2. Drop in the butter, once it melts add the garlic and cook for about 30 seconds while stirring frequently to prevent the garlic from burning.

3. Add the broccoli, water, salt, and pepper. Close the lid, secure the pressure valve, and select Pressure mode on High pressure for about 5 minutes.

4. Press the Start/Stop button. Once the cooking time is up, do a quick pressure release/

5. Use a stick blender to mash the ingredients until smooth to your desired consistency and well combined.

6. Stir in Cream cheese and adjust the taste with salt and pepper. Close the crisping lid and cook for about 2 minutes on Broil function.

7. Serve warm.

Chipotle Vegetarian Chili

Preparation time: 15 minutes

Cooking time: 30 minutes

Overall time: 45 minutes

Serves: 2 to 4 people

Recipe Ingredients:

- 1 (28 oz.) can of diced tomatoes
- 3 chipotle peppers; chopped
- 3 garlic cloves, minced
- 1 (15 oz.) can of black beans, rinsed and drained
- 1/4 cup of fresh parsley; chopped
- 2 cups of carrots; chopped
- 1 cup of red lentils
- 1 cup of red quinoa
- 2 cups of cashews; chopped
- 1 cup of onion; chopped
- 4½ cups of water
- 2 tablespoons of chili powder
- 1 teaspoon of salt

Cooking Instructions:

1. In the pot, mix tomatoes, onion, chipotle peppers, chili powder, lentils, walnuts, carrots, quinoa, garlic, and salt; stir in more water.

2. Seal the pressure lid, choose Pressure, set to High, and set the timer to 30 minutes. Press the Start button.

3. When ready, release the pressure quickly. Into the chili, add black beans; simmer on Keep Warm until heated through.

4. Add 1 cup of water if you want a thinner consistency. Top with a garnish of parsley.

Tasty Acorn Squash

Preparation time: 10 minutes

Cooking time: 20 minutes

Overall time: 30 minutes

Serves: 2 to 4 people

Recipe Ingredients:

- 1 pound of acorn squash, peeled and cut into chunks /450g
- ½ cup of water /125ml
- 2 tablespoons of butter /30g
- 1 tablespoon of dark brown sugar /15g
- 1 tablespoon of cinnamon /15g
- 3 tablespoons of honey; divided 45ml
- Salt and ground black pepper to taste

Cooking Instructions:

1. In a small bowl, mix 1 tbsp honey and water; pour into the pressure cooker's pot.

2. Add in squash. Seal the and cook on High pressure for about 4 minutes. Press the Start button. When ready, release the pressure quickly.

3. Transfer the squash to a serving dish. Turn Foodi to Sear/Sauté. Mix brown sugar, cinnamon, the remaining 2 tablespoon of honey and the liquid in the pot.

4. Cook as you stir for about 4 minutes to obtain a thick consistency and starts to turn caramelized and golden.

5. Spread honey glaze over squash; add pepper and salt for seasoning.

Acknowledgement

In preparing the "Complete Ninja Foodi Cookbook for Two", I sincerely wish to acknowledge my indebtedness to my husband for his support and the wholehearted cooperation and vast experience of my two colleagues - Mrs. Alexandra Bryne and Mrs. Barbara Miles.

Emily Cook